Vladim.
Ph.D. (in biology)

Anatomy of God

(Collected Articles)

Translated from Russian
by Vladimir Antonov
and Anton Teplyy
Correctors of the English translation —
Hiero Nani and Keenan Murphy

2nd new edition,
with corrected very gross mistakes
made by the previous translator
and supplemented

2012

ISBN 9781453752043

This book is a compilation of articles by scientist-biologist Dr. Vladimir Antonov, who dedicated his life to studying, among other things, non-material forms of life and people's relations with them.

Among non-material forms of life, the most important for us are the Representatives of the Primordial Consciousness (of the Creator, of God-the-Father) — the Holy Spirits.

Learning from Them allowed us to formulate clear and reasonable answers to some of the most important questions: what is God, what is man, what is the meaning of our lives on the Earth and how can we realize it most successfully, and what should be our relationships with God.

The book can be interesting and useful to every one of us, including pedagogues and the youth.

Contents

www.swami-center.org
www.spiritual-art.info

Anatomy of God

On our planet there are many variations in the understanding of the nature of God, of the meaning of our lives and ways of its realization. Different concepts emerged and gave birth to different religious associations of people.

Another important point here is that with time people tend to distort the original truths received from God by substituting them with fantasies or by changing them to fit people's selfish desires.

Why does it happen? We discussed this topic in detail in book [13]. In brief, I can say that the reason here consists in the great spectrum of differences between people, in terms of their intellectual and moral levels. The most striking religious perversions occurred in cases when power was seized by aggressive primitives... This resulted in inquisitions, crusades, and various kinds of fundamentalism, where the followers were taught to seek salvation through, for example, the killing of infidels...

But all this does not mean that religion caused nothing but harm to humankind. In different times in different countries there were the Representatives of the Creator, Who brought to people the Truth in its original purity [8]. People of primitive nature quite often tortured and killed these Divine Teachers, sincerely believing that thus they "protected the purity of faith" — their "faith" of primitives...

* * *

Another important reason for the fading out of the epicenters of higher religious knowledge consists in the fact that in the past on the Earth there were no advanced means of imparting and preserving intellectual information. In the distant past people tried to write down their thoughts on stone tablets, on papyrus, etc. This is why the subsequent generations could not become acquainted with the records made by Thoth-the-Atlantean (Hermes Trismegistus), by Pythagoras, and by other Great Ones. And even the technology of printing on paper could not solve this problem completely, so that people of different countries and speaking in different languages could exchange important information quickly and easily.

At present time this task is solved thanks to the Internet and to other computer technologies. These modern technologies together with the knowledge about God accumulated by scientists, who have dedicated their lives to this task, have created the necessary prerequisites for forming the all-mankind repository of knowledge containing fundamental information about the nature of God and man, and about how we should live on the Earth to realize successfully God's intent for us.

* * *

We are not going to list and analyze here various folklore (naive, fairy-tale, pagan) ideas about God that existed and exist now in different nations. Let us begin straight away with expounding the most principal knowledge.

It is appropriate to begin this topic with discussing the multidimensionality of space. After all, it is not mathematical reasoning but physical reality!

Let us imagine a multi-layered pie. The layers of multidimensionality, in contrast to the usual pie, differ among themselves not by the height of their location but by their place on the scale of energetical *subtlety-coarseness*. This is the scale of multidimensionality. The most subtle layer of the universal "pie" is the Primordial Consciousness, which is called in different human languages as the Creator, God-the-Father, Jehovah, Allah, Ishvara, Tao, etc. On the opposite end of this scale there is hell

— the "rubbish heap" of the evolutionary Process. Between the Primordial Consciousness and hell there are other layers. Among them are those containing "building material" for formation of matter (protoprakriti) and for formation of souls (protopurusha). These eons also should be cognized on the Path to Mergence with the Creator. They can be discovered when one learns to cross the *Mirror*, and this is possible only if one does it from the cleansed and well-developed anahata chakra.

I can give another example to help understand the nature of multidimensionality.

Let us imagine a glass aquarium. Its main visible content is water. But in it, there is also light, which almost does not interact with the water. Also there are the energies of radio waves, which transmit information to radio receivers and to televisions. There are also the energies of the gravitational fields of the Earth, of the Sun, and of the Moon; there are neutrinos and other flows of energies, invisible to the bodies' eyes…

And they are present not only inside the aquarium: they are present everywhere!

In order to explain this phenomenon to children, one can give them a portable radio receiver attuned to a certain radio frequency, which they can carry inside their homes or take outside. Thus children can see that the electromagnetic field, which ensures the receiving of radio waves, exists not only in the point where the receiver was attuned to them, but everywhere in the space around them, even outdoors.

Moreover, one can demonstrate to children that similar fields, corresponding to other radio frequencies, are present as well, and that they do not hinder each other but exist as if in their own layers of space, invisible to our eyes.

This example can be a good analogy for understanding the essence of the layers of multidimensionality.

It is the same with real multidimensional space: spatial dimensions (which are called *eons* in Greek or *lokas* in Sanskrit) with their inhabitants (spirits of different levels of development and God) are present everywhere. We are used to looking only at the material plane of our existence and do not notice them. But the inhabitants of these eons see us and therefore can influence us. (Apostle Philip depicted this situation in His Gospel [8]).

Phenomena taking place in dimensions other than the material plane cannot be seen or studied by the organs of sense of our bodies or with the help of some material tools: there is no way to move our bodies or tools there! But they can be studied very well with the consciousness developed to the necessary level.

This does not concern the use of psychodelics, which destroy both the body and the soul! (Among followers of drug addicts there is an opinion that such substances allow one to exit into the astral plane and to study the non-material eons in this way. In reality, in such a case, one explores only one eon, usually the eon of hell. In this situation, one cannot move from one eon to another, up to the Abode of the Primordial Consciousness. No self-development is possible in this case; there can only be degradation.)

The correct researching activity has to be performed with the fully clear self-awareness — through the stages of ethical and energetical purification, and then through development of the consciousness with the help of the methods of its refinement and growth. All this is described in the book [9], in our other books, and demonstrated in our films-lectures. Now let me just stress that one cannot achieve success in this work without putting emphasis on the development of oneself as a spiritual heart. There is no other possibility.

* * *

Only primitive religious concepts depict God in the forms of a human or animal! In reality, God — in the aspects of the Absolute and the Primordial Consciousness — is infinite in size and eternal. His scale is the scale of the entire universe!

The main part of God, which is called the Primordial Consciousness or the *Heart of the Absolute*, can be likened to a boundless ocean. He is a boundless Ocean of Living Subtlest Consciousness existing in the deepest loka, which is called the Abode of the Primordial Consciousness. His state there can be described as Calm.

He is not a Personality. He is the Whole of All Those Who have achieved the Perfection and have merged with Him. In this sense, He is the *United We*, as He Himself asserts [8].

… Love is the emotion that helps souls to merge with each other.

Having learned to love other people and all the living in the Creation, as well as the Creation in general, and having developed ourselves as love, we can then direct our love towards the Creator. At this point we become refined and well-developed — in the quantitative aspect — spiritual hearts. And then we flow into Him and merge with Him in the Embrace of Love!

This is not a beautiful fantasy or allegory. This is the Reality for all Souls Who have achieved this.

In particular, it was described by Apostle Philip, a personal disciple of Jesus Christ, in His Gospel [8]. Philip — together with Jesus and some other Apostles of Jesus — is now an Integral Part of the *United We*.

One can find the same concept in the Quran: addressing Muhammad, God speaks about Himself using two pronouns — *I* and *We*…

Yes, He says that He is the *Higher I*, the *United I*, the *United We*. All this is true.

It is also important to note that although we use the masculine form when speaking about the Creator, the *United We* is composed of Divine Representatives of both sexes — according to Their last Incarnations.

... For those who are used to regarding themselves and others only as material bodies it may be hard to imagine how one can be the *United We*. But, verily, man is not a body! Man is a self-aware energy, which is called consciousness or soul! The body is but a temporary dwelling given to every one of us for our development during the time of incarnation. The body is as if a machine that allows the soul to act, to learn, and to grow in the world of matter. And this machine is controlled by man himself, first of all.

After disincarnation, all people cognize the reality of being a soul. But one can gain this knowledge without ceasing the incarnate existence. One can achieve this by developing oneself through the methods of Buddhi Yoga.

... In the Abode of the *United We*, there is blissful Calm. There, all the Consciousnesses are merged into One. Intensive Light and Light-Fire are manifested only as a result of Intentions directed to the Creation and Actions performed within it.

The *United We* possesses all the fullness of the Divine Power, Which can be manifested, in particular, in control over matter, in materialization and dematerialization, and in transformation of matter.

Embodied spiritual Masters, Who have become well established in the Mergence with the *United We*, can manifest Themselves as Great Divine Wonder-Workers.

Being incarnate or non-incarnate, They can come out from Their common Abode and create *working sites* where They work with incarnate people. There each One of Them teaches, among other things, meditative methods to incarnate spiritual seekers who have developed the ability to perceive God directly.

Such Representatives of the Primordial Consciousness (of the *United We*) are called Holy Spirits. In the aggregate sense, They are called the *Holy Spirit* or *Brahman*.

It is also appropriate to discuss here the concept of *Trinity*.

What concerns God-the-Father, we have talked about already.

We have also explained what the Holy Spirit is.

And every One of the incarnate Representatives of God-the-Father is called Avatar, Christ, or Messiah (these words from different languages mean the same).[1]

This is what Trinity is.

Now let us discuss the term *Absolute*.

Sathya Sai Baba once told us on behalf of the *United We:* "The Earth is a Manifestation of My Beingness".

Yes, the planet where we are born and live is a multidimensional conglomeration. Its matter and material objects are one of the components of this conglomeration. *Deeper* in the scale of multidimensionality there are other eons, including the Abode of the Primordial Consciousness.

From the depths of multidimensionality, the Earth is seen as a structure consisting of Divine Light; it is only its outer layer (crust) that is dense and solid. Such a structure can be likened to a bud on a tree. The bud originates from the substance of the tree; it is not completely inde-

---

[1] They all teach the same truths to people. But people distort Their Teachings thus beginning to wage wars among themselves because of arising differences. Members of every party in such a war believe that they "protect the true faith". But the Knowledge taught by all the Representatives of the Creator is one and universal.

pendent, not existing on its own. Despite the fact that the structure of the bud's tissues differ from the structure of the tissues of its parent's substance, the bud and the tree are one.

It is the same with conglomerations of planets and stars: they do not exist on their own, but are "buds" of the Creation produced by the Creator.

It is in this sense that one speaks about God as about the Absolute: the Absolute is *Absolutely Everything*, the Creator coessential with His Creation.

* * *

In this article we have to discuss one more subject: Fiery and Light Divine Manifestations.

Representatives of the *United We* come out with Parts of Themselves from Their common Abode — to Their *working sites* on the surface of the planet in slightly different ways. Some of Them do it being fully transparent Consciousnesses; They are, for example, Huang Di, Apostle Philip, Gautama Buddha. Others create at Their *working sites* Mahadoubles: giant anthropomorphic Forms consisting of the most tender Living Light. Such are most of Them (according to our observations). Others yet, in addition to manifesting Themselves in the form of Mahadoubles, create forms shining with bright Light-Fire, resembling the usual Sun seen from the Earth.

Jesus calls such Representatives of the Primordial Consciousness Who look like the Sun — bright, intense, stationary with regards to the Earth's surface — "Suns of God" [17]. Their color can vary from light-goldish — to orange tint (in the case of Surya) or to reddish tint (in the case of Sarkar). Apart from the two mentioned Representatives of the Creator, we observed "Suns of God" created by Jesus, by His Apostles Mark and John, also by Sathya Sai Baba, Eagle, Assyris, Odin, Adler, Bartholomew, Ptahhotep, Larisa, Sulia, Lada, Yamamata.[2]

... Every One of the Holy Spirits can have several *working sites*, which are sometimes situated thousands of kilometers from each other.

Today we have a unique possibility for studying such an activity of Divine Teachers, because Sathya Sai Baba has a material body in His Indian Ashram. This allows us to observe hidden aspects of the work of this Great Avatar of our time, the structure of how He distributes Himself for the sake of helping incarnate people.

He comes out from the Abode of the *United We* as a giant "Sun of God" shining from His Ashram. This is the center of His activity on the Earth. From here He stretches His numerous Divine Arms to many places on the surface of our planet. These Arms pass through the Ocean of the *United We* like underground fiery riverbeds. They end at His larger or smaller *working sites*, where His Mahadoubles are present; and we know at least one of His *working sites* where His "Sun of God" is too.

"Suns of God" are sometimes seen as if behind the horizon, but most often they appear to a certain degree above the surface of the Earth.

"Suns of God" are boundary structures formed at places where some Representatives of the Primordial Consciousness come out from Their Abode.

"Suns of God" is one of the manifestations of the Divine *Fire*. (The latter can exist in forms other than "Suns of God").

The Divine *Fire* created by Holy Spirits or by Avatars can be used by us for purification and healing of our bodies and for divinizing the matter of our bodies. This *Fire* is not burning for those who progress successfully

---

[2] You can read about Them and about other Representatives of the Creator know to us in [8].

on the Path to Perfection. But hellish souls (incarnate and non-incarnate) cannot withstand It.

True spiritual warriors can place themselves in the Divine *Fire* not only as souls but also together with their bodies — if there is a "Sun of God" available for such work. In this case they can, among other things, purify their bodies — with the help of the hands of the consciousness — from all energies coarser than the Divine *Fire*. Thanks to this work, bodies with their energies are purified, healed, transformed. From fully purified bodies it is much easier to enter the Divine eons. (On the contrary, this is impossible to do from bodies contaminated with coarse energies).

But it is even more prospective to become "Suns of God" ourselves.

It is for this purpose that we were embodied on the Earth! This is why God sent us here!

Let us ask ourselves: does my current way of life conform to this Path?

And we have to remember that one should begin self-transformation from the very beginning! Where is the beginning? — One has to find it on one's own by studying in detail the materials listed in the end of this book.

* * *

To beg salvation from God is a completely meaningless thing. Jesus Christ teaches that everyone has to cognize and master the Abode of the Creator with his or her own efforts (Matt 11:12; Luke 16:16).

He also commanded: "Become perfect as your Heavenly Father is perfect!" (Matt 5:48). And "Learn (this) from Me!" (Matt 11:29).

Yes, Jesus and all the Holy Spirits are glad to help every incarnate person, but this person should also make efforts on self-development!

And there is no reason for us to regard God as our Servant who allegedly has to indulge us and save us, while we continue to live in our vices!

God, looking at people begging salvation from Him, may ask: how can one save them? They do nothing to be saved! They do not follow Our recommendations — despite all Our efforts, despite, in particular, the self-sacrificial Feat of Jesus Christ Who gave to people the Teachings about the Path to Our Abode! And only in this Abode one finds the true and final Salvation! By the way, is parasitism a quality that should be encouraged in people? No! They have to work on themselves! Only to such people We give Our help in abundance!

The author of this book took heed of this truth several tens of years ago — and accepted God as his Teacher. He managed to *save* himself and helped many others on this path.

… It is much more difficult to pave a way than to go by an already paved road! The road has been paved for you now! You just need to learn "the rules of the road" and to begin moving forward!…

Straight Path to Achieving Spiritual Perfection

Many years of hard work of us — a group of scientists who studied the multidimensional space of the universe and the forms of consciousness that inhabit its layers (eons, lokas) — allowed us to reach a full understanding of the most important things that should be laid in the foundation of the outlook of every modern person. This knowledge gives complete answers to the fundamental philosophical questions: what is man, what is the nature of the Divine, what should be the relationships between man and God, and what is the meaning of our lives and how to realize it. We described it in many publications where this knowledge is expounded in a simple language, which is easy to understand for any intellectually developed person.

In particular, during our work in this direction, we learned from many Divine Teachers — Representatives of the Primordial Consciousness (God-the-Father, the Creator). Among Them are Jesus Christ and some of His Apostles, as well as Krishna, Huang-Di, Odin, Babaji from Haidakhan, Sathya Sai Baba, and many Others. Some of Them are widely known now; Others are known only to relatively small groups of people incarnate at present; some Others left no noticeable traces in history [8].

What do They have in common that allows us to regard Them as Divine? The Apostle Philip — a personal disciple of Jesus Christ — wrote about this in His Gospel [8]. Namely, all of Them found in the past the Way to the Abode of the Primordial Universal Consciousness, established Themselves in Mergence with It, and became Its Integral Parts.

There are also differences among Them. For example, Divine Teachers can be distinguished by the subtlest shades of Their Divine Love. They also differ by the "age" of living in the Abode of the Primordial Consciousness: personal development of every Divine Individual does not end with attainment of Divinity but continues. God told us about this in the following way: "There is a long way from a seed that sprouted up and rooted in Me — to the Universal Tree that gives life to all the living".

... From the standpoint of the methodology of spiritual development, it is important to choose from the vast number of true and false methods of spiritual development known to people — only the really significant, which really allow man to advance quickly to Divinity and to become a Part of the Primordial Consciousness.

To us, possessing vast experience of living communication with the Inhabitants of the highest eon of the multidimensional space and with the representatives of the other eons, it is absolutely evident that only those people who choose the Path of the Spiritual Heart have chances of attaining spiritual Perfection in Mergence with the Primordial Consciousness relatively quickly. In other words, only Those Who have developed Themselves, during the incarnate state, as great and Divinely subtle Spiritual Hearts, appear among the achieved Ones. They are Those Who constitute, in aggregate, the *United We* of the Creator.

... Let us consider the main stages of the spiritual Path in more detail.

First, we have to accept and realize in life the basic ethical principles suggested to us by God:

— Refusal of all forms of causing unnecessary harm to other creatures, including plants. In particular, the principle given to us through Moses "You shall not kill!" has to be extended not only to killing people but to killing animals and to unnecessary killing plants.

— Taking care of others, striving to help everyone selflessly in everything good. It is through selfless (and unobtrusive) help to others, that we not only learn psychological peculiarities of other people and become "soul-knowers", but also develop love in ourselves. "God is Love," taught Jesus Christ. This means, in particular, that in order to approach God we have to develop in ourselves this quality first of all.

But what is love? Love is the whole spectrum of corresponding emotional states. And one can develop them both through "usual" methods (emotional attunement to the harmony of nature and to adequate works of art[3], interactions with harmonious people and animals, har-

---

[3] http://ecopsychology.swami-center.org/art-and-spiritual-development.shtml

monious sexual interaction devoid of egoism, etc.) and through special spiritual exercises that directly develop the organ of emotional love — the spiritual heart. Such special methods allow worthy people to accelerate their personal evolution by thousands of times and to attain Perfection in their current incarnations. This, of course, gives them the possibility of helping incarnate beings — from their new status — much more efficiently.

Among other important ethical principles, one should mention the following:

— introducing into one's own life the awareness of the priority of the spiritual evolution — contrary to the tendency to compete in interactions with people and to the desire to possess superfluous (for the spiritual Path) earthly boons,

— refusal of coarse emotional states; the control of emotions is easily achieved with the help of the system of methods of psychical self-regulation developed by us [9].

... So, the spiritual heart developed to the cosmic scales is the foundation of man's spiritual advancement. In the Abode of the Creator, there are no souls who came there in any other way, for example, those who put emphasis on the development of the power or intellectual aspects. Both these aspects are also important, but should play only a supplementary role.

Development of the spiritual heart begins in the anahata chakra through its cleansing and extending to the size of the chest, at least.

Then the growth of the spiritual heart continues outside the body. This process is more successful if special meditative training at appropriate *places of power* is used.

Growth of the spiritual heart is proportional to development of subtle (not coarse) *power* of the individual consciousness. Those who successfully develop themselves in this direction, gradually gain the ability to live not in the material body but to be spiritual hearts which are thousands or millions of times larger than our material bodies. This allows, in particular, moving easily through multidimensional space and exploring it by crossing the borders between these eons. One does this with full self-awareness and control of one's own states and also the place of one's staying; psychodelic drugs, which destroy the body and soul, are not needed for this purpose at all.

At these stages of development, the consciousness of man is enriched with the Kundalini energy — an individual reserve of Atmic energy accumulated in the past. This allows one, in particular, to form a Dharmakaya — a huge and subtle body of consciousness consisting of all 3 dantians. And the chakras then merge with the Primordial Consciousness.

At the same time, one needs training in *dissolving* oneself-consciousness in the highest (subtlest) eons. This is known as attainment of Nirodhi — one of the Nirvanic states.

Thanks to such practices, man easily masters not only life in paradise (one of the subtle eons of multidimensional space) but also in the three "behind-the-Mirror" (akashic) eons, including the eon of protomatter (protoprakriti), the eon filled with the "building material" for souls (protopurusha), and the Atmic eon of Chidakasha.

Self-perfecting has to include many other aspects of development of the individual consciousness, including intellectual and power ones. Serving other incarnate beings through helping them also contributes to this.

Through the methods of the spiritual work mentioned above, one can easily develop the ability to communicate with the Holy Spirits, with Jesus Christ. Jesus and other Representatives of the Creator become our personal Teachers and guide us to God-the-Father, into His Abode.

In the language tradition used by Krishna, which was introduced later into the lexicon of Buddhists, one may say that in this way people of both sexes, who are well prepared by their past experience, easily achieve the Nirvana in Brahman (the Holy Spirit), the Nirvana in Ishvara (God-the-Father), and Nirvana in the Absolute.

As for the Islamic tradition, we gave a full explanation of the nature of Allah (the Creator, Primordial Consciousness) Who told about Himself, through Muhammad, as "I" and as "We". After all, Allah is not a Personality, but an Aggregation of Personalities merged together. Of course, there are also His Individual Manifestations.

Now one may better understand the methodology of the *Straight Path* mentioned in the Quran — the Path of cognition of Allah and Merging with Him through humble and faithful love. One may find more details about this in [8], where Sufi Grand Master and other Great Sufis speak about the *Straight Path*.

... Materials of book [8], compiled from the sayings of the Representatives of the Creator Who attained Divine Perfection through different religious traditions, clearly demonstrate that God is one for all people (though people call Him differently in different languages) and that the methodology of attainment of spiritual Self-Realization is also one.

It is demonstrated especially brightly by the biographies of Those Adepts Who successfully finished Their "inner jihad" (holy war for the Perfection) being embodied in Atlantis, in Africa, in Southeast Asia, among American Indians, in the countries of European culture, in Russia.

It should be emphasized that success on the spiritual Path is achieved neither through inventing "gods" and then worshipping them, nor through rituals and endless panhandling before God, but through real efforts on transforming oneself as a soul, as a consciousness. Such a transformation has to begin from ethics; otherwise God does not allow us to approach Him!

... You can try using this knowledge given to us by Divine Teachers, though we cannot promise that traversing this Path will be necessarily easy for you... Yet, if man manages to traverse even a significant part of this Path during the time remaining in the current incarnation — this will ensure favorable conditions in the future unfoldment of one's destiny.

Also, let us pay attention to the importance of teaching the basics of this knowledge to children, namely the ideas of ethics, responsibility for one's own deeds, words, and even thoughts — before God, Who waits for us to become like Him — perfect Love, perfect Wisdom, and perfect Power!

Three Stages of Centering on the Path of Spiritual Self-Realization

Many years ago we created a 20-hour video film that was titled *Three Steps of Centering*. However, since then many technical advancements have been made in the field of video production; therefore, unfortunately, this film is now out of date due to its old technical quality.

Yet we ourselves have managed to make significant progress in gaining knowledge and experience on the Path of spiritual development. So it makes sense now to discuss this subject again — at the current new cycle of its development.

It is not necessary to describe all the numerous nuances of the spiritual Path in this short article. Let us just point out basic milestones for the travelers. One can continue the research with the help of the literature given at the end of this book.

Stage 1

In any country and in any large town people differ significantly among themselves. This concerns not sexual or national differences. The main difference here is the quality of incarnate souls according to their evolutionary age and according to what qualities these people have developed during the time of their incarnations.

Some people are only capable of leading a way of life which is not much better that the life of animals, and sometimes people lead lives that are even worse. Such people are driven by emotions of aggression, envy, greed, lust (egoistic sexual desires), revenge, jealousy, etc. If they come to a religious environment, they can only beg from God forgiveness for their real or imaginary vices, to participate in alleged "saving" rituals, to take part in feasts (to drink heavily) when celebrating certain events from history. And if they are influenced by strong personalities (quite often of devilish nature), they then join masses of religious fanatics who are similar to gangs of rowdy football fans or to functionaries of criminal political regimes...[4]

---

[4] There is a whole range of intellectual levels of people: from almost zero intelligence up to genius abilities and higher [5, 8,13].

It is determined mainly by the fact that the intellectual function of the soul develops not in one but in many incarnations.

Also, physicians found out a long time ago that in cases of alcoholics and other drug addicts there is a high risk of birth of children with a defective intellect.

And one should understand that God does not incarnate promising souls into an environment unfavorable for spiritual development.

In medicine of the past centuries there was the term physiological silliness. What did it mean?

There was a division of human silliness into two levels: pathological silliness, which is called also oligophrenia, and physi-

Completely different from them are people possessing an intellect developed in the process of their personal evolution. They are, for example, true scientists (contrary to those who come to the scientific field by chance), writers, people of art, journalists, successful businessmen and politicians.

Such people do not accept primitive religious forms. Therefore many of them live as atheists — until they encounter a wise religious-philosophical concept.[5]

---

ological silliness. The latter was peculiar to too many so-called "normal" people, and therefore physicians did not want to call all of them mentally ill.

Oligophrenic persons were subdivided into three groups according to the level of the pathology: idiots (those with the least pronounced feeblemindedness), imbeciles, and morons.

And the physiologically silly are the closest to morons group of "normal" people, who do not consider themselves silly at all.

One can observe (or at least imagine) what are the levels of understanding of the religious path by the representatives of each of these four mentioned groups, and by those who do not belong to them.

In the current century as well, we can observe in different countries mass religious forms established and supported by those physiologically silly.

It is clear that there is no reason to fight against this phenomenon with force: it naturally corresponds to the needs and possibilities of a significant part of the society.

But wise leaders could contribute to introducing into the mentality of human masses reasonable religious-philosophical knowledge. This could begin with including it into educational programs and promoting it through mass media.

And, of course, it is extremely unreasonable to encourage feeblemindedness in people by promoting feebleminded concepts.

[5] However, not all atheists are so because of the lack of sound religious-philosophical concepts, but some simply prefer to live without feeling personal responsibility before Living God.

Yes, there are people with a developed intellect who are capable of mastering the stages of the spiritual Path successfully. On the other hand, without a developed intellect, one cannot comprehend even the basics of ethics. And for those people, the Creator does not allow approaching Him!

... The intellectually developed person can discover true religious-philosophical knowledge, become acquainted with it, and accept the principles of life on the Earth suggested to us by God. Then such a person can begin to master the first stage of psycho-energetical development. This stage implies development of oneself as a spiritual heart.

... In the human organism there are seven bioenergetical organs which are called chakras.

The most important of them is the central chakra anahata located in the chest. It is the organ responsible for producing the entire spectrum of the emotions of love.

Above the anahata there is the neck chakra vishuddha responsible for the esthetical appraisal of situations.

Above it, in the head, there are two chakras (ajna and sahasrara) responsible for intellectual functions.

Below the anahata, in the upper half of the abdomen, there is the manipura chakra. Its function consists in providing energy for the organism.

In the lower half of the abdomen, there is the svadhisthana chakra that produces, among other things, sexual emotions.

And in the lower part of the pelvis, there is the muladhara chakra, whose function consists in taking part in accumulating the energy of the organism. (For more details about the chakras see [9]).

All the chakras are necessary. There are no good or bad chakras. It is desirable that all the chakras be purified from energetical contamination and developed.

Another chakra, which is very important on the spiritual Path, — the sahasrara located in the top part of the head at the place of the cerebral hemispheres. A high level of development of this chakra signifies one's large intellectual potential, which is very important for successful spiritual development.

But for further spiritual advancement, such a person has to abandon the tendency of centering oneself in the head and has to begin to center the consciousness in the anahata chakra.

It is in this way all true spiritual seekers from different religious movements, including Christians-Hesychasts, achieved success [9].

It is possible to say that those, who have mastered centering themselves in the anahatas, have mastered the first principal stage of the spiritual Path.

This achievement is significant not only for advancement to spiritual heights. *Anahatic* qualities of a person allow him or her to continue living in harmony, in a happy state — independent of the circumstances. For most people,[6] it is pleasant to communicate with such a person. They become the sources of spiritual light for others! They also become invincible to diseases, which plague those who always live in negative emotions.

… The Creator is the most subtle form of consciousness.

Opposite of Him are inhabitants of hell, which is the "rubbish heap" of the evolutionary Process. They are the most coarse concerning their energetical status, which has been developed by them during their incarnations.

So the Path to the Creator implies, among other things, refinement of the consciousness. How can one do it? — Through one's control over emotions with the help of the art of psychical self-regulation [9].

Let me explain that emotions are states of the consciousnesses (souls). And after the death of the material

---

[6] Except for hellish persons who hate everyone around.

bodies, we continue to live in the state which was most habitual for us during the incarnate lives. In this way we predetermine ourselves to living either in hell or in paradise!

This is one of the reasons why working with the anahata chakra is so important. In this chakra, no coarse emotional states can occur; it produces only subtle emotions of love: emotions of tenderness, care, gratitude, reverence, etc.

And if we live constantly in this chakra, we can easily rid ourselves of all coarse emotional states and habituate ourselves to subtle ones.

Moreover, it is the emotions of love that can bring souls to mutual mergence. By learning love in contacts with such objects of the Creation as: other people, animals, plants, living nature, etc. — we prepare ourselves for the Mergence with the Divine Souls — the Holy Spirits and then with the entire Primordial Consciousness.

Stage 2

On the spiritual Path we have to strive to achieve the level of subtlety of the Primordial Consciousness. Also we need power of the refined consciousness, which is important for the soul to be able to actively act inside and outside its current material body. Without this power one cannot even move from one spatial dimension to another, say nothing of staying in other dimensions. And the power of an individual consciousness depends directly on the size of the consciousness.

How can one become a great soul (mahatma) during the current incarnation in a reasonable period of time? Only with the help of special training of oneself-consciousness.

The spiritual heart is a structure of the consciousness that can begin to grow inside the anahata chakra if there are conditions favorable for this. Further efforts on a) developing the spiritual heart, and then b) developing oneself as a spiritual heart — allows one to outgrow the anahata chakra in size, then the entire material body, and then one can grow more and more — up to infinity...

What do such trainings consist in? In the beginning, if we have mastered the chakra anahata, we can learn to push its walls from inside with the hands of the consciousness. Then we can learn to fill "cocoons" of energetically subtle and powerful plants (*plants of power*). Then — to fill in the same manner the Forms of Consciousnesses of our Divine Teachers — the Holy Spirits — at Their *working sites*.

It is clear that for perceiving Them and communicating successfully with Them, we need to refine the consciousness to the necessary level.

Holy Spirits, penetrating easily — in Their eon — through the matter of the Earth and through any material objects, come out from Their Abode and manifest Themselves for incarnate people in the form of Mahadoubles: giant anthropomorphic Forms consisting of subtle flame-like Light. These Mahadoubles can be from tens of meters up to kilometers in height; Their width at the level of the ground ranges from several meters to kilometers.

If we have learned to merge with Them by entering Their Forms, we can grow as consciousnesses with Their help inside these Forms.

Many Divine Teachers are ready to help us in this growth: Jesus Christ and His Apostles, Krishna, Babaji from Haidakhan, Sathya Sai Baba, Ptahhotep, Elisabeth Haich, Ngomo, Pythagoras, Thoth-the-Atlantean, Adler and many Others [5-6,8-9]. But let me repeat that we have to prepare ourselves for this, so that we become able to see Them and to communicate with Them as easily as we communicate with incarnate people.

... And then the question is: how can we cognize the Creator?

One of the ways to realization of this goal consists in settling oneself (as a consciousness developed as a spiritual heart) in the core of our planet.

The Fiery core of the Earth is that part of the planet which is most close — in the corresponding eon — to the state of the Creator. It is as if a connection link between the Creator and this element of His Creation (planet Earth). And it can serve us as a passage to the Abode of the Primordial Consciousness.

The criterion of success in this work is the ability to feel the center of oneself in the core of the planet. This would mean that one has mastered the second stage of centering.

... One has to begin mastering the core with filling — with oneself-consciousness — our entire multidimensional planet — in its subtlest light-filled components, first of all.

Having cognized thus our planet through love for it and mergence with it, we can feel then very well the entire scale of multidimensionality: from the boundary with hell — up to the subtlety found in the planet's core. If we have mastered this, it would be easy for us to submerge into the Abode of the Creator. Thus we begin the direct cognition of the main Goal of our existence, the main Goal of all our spiritual efforts.

Yet I have to warn you against the illusion which our imagination can create: one has to understand clearly that the distance to the core of our planet is measured by thousands of kilometers. Therefore it makes sense to ask oneself honestly: can I really expand the consciousness to such a distance now? Or do I first need to continue growing as a spiritual heart, for example in the expanse over the sea, in the expanse of the steppe, in the majestic expanse seen from the peaks of mountains?

Stage 3

The third stage of centering implies fullness of Mergence with the Creator, which enables one to feel the center of oneself in His Abode. And all the rest existing in other eons is located as if around and outside this Center[7].

Let me note that the Creator calls Himself the *Heart of the Absolute*.

Moving from the second stage to the fullness of mastering of the third stage, requires, at least, years of unceasing spiritual efforts. It does not make sense to speak much about them in this article: those who have reached this summit are guided further by God.

But I want to mention two very important aspects of work at this stage:

The first one is the ability to enter the state of Mergence with the Divine Consciousness. The path to gaining this ability begins with developing in oneself a very important ethical quality called *lowliness of mind* — lowly, humble feeling of oneself. If one has not developed this quality, he or she has no chances for spiritual success.

Let me also note that Jesus Christ attached much importance to this![8]

I should also stress that the true lowliness of mind (contrary to its false imitations) can be gained only after mastering the first stage of centering.

One also strengthens the skills of Mergence with the help of special trainings in mastering the state of *non-I*. In this state the feeling of oneself is merged completely

---

[7] It is important to understand that here we speak about multidimensional space, not about a plane-like one.

[8] This principle is mentioned in almost every book listed in the bibliography.

with the object of one's love. And this object, in the end, has to be our Creator.

The second aspect is the necessity of developing the *arms of the consciousness*, which grow from the spiritual heart and are coessential to it. It is best to develop the strength of these arms by giving through them the power of one's love — first to some particular incarnate beings, then to whole parts of our planet with all the beings living on them, and then by permeating with these arms the layers of the Absolute surrounding the *Heart of the Absolute*.

One can find more details about mastering this stage in the historical spiritual classics [8]. For example, one has to master mergence of oneself — simultaneously with *That Which Is Above* and with *That Which Is Below*, as it was recommended by Hermes Trismegistus in the *Emerald Tablet* [8].

Jiva and Buddhi

Jiva is the Sanskrit equivalent of the word *soul*.

In its incarnate state, the jiva is attached to its material body. It lives in the body and perceives the world with the help of the body's organs of sense; it thinks with the help of the body's brain. This is why it is so difficult for embodied people to disidentify themselves — even mentally — with the body and the mind (*manas* in Sanskrit).

When the material body dies, the jiva continues to live in non-material spatial dimensions: some jivas live in the eons of hell, some live in the paradisiacal abodes. This depends on the state of the consciousness one got used to living in during one's incarnate life. After the death of the body, those, accustomed to coarse (i.e. hellish) states of the consciousness, continue to live in these states among other souls similar to them; this is what hell is. Those who have accustomed themselves to life in subtle and tender states, who have ridden themselves of anger and other kinds of emotional coarseness — they appear in paradise. Also we should remember that in most cases life in non-incarnate states is much longer than life in material bodies.

What is the purpose of these incarnations? Can the only purpose here consist in the idea that a terrifying and fearsome God-Judge sorts us out between hell and paradise after the death of our bodies? Nonsense! Yet this is a belief of the followers of many primitive religious movements!

No, in reality the Creator incarnates us in His Creation so that we may develop ourselves intellectually, ethically, aesthetically, develop the power aspect, and master in all fullness the complex of emotions that are called in general by the word LOVE. The latter is the most important thing!

Depending on whether we master it well or poorly, the Creator (through Holy Spirits) forms our future destinies (karma), which are perceived by most people either as good or bad. Good destiny is when He creates pleasant conditions for us for continuing our self-development. Bad destiny is created by Him so that we, having appeared in unpleasant conditions, begin to seek the way out (this concerns our worldview, first of all), so that we may understand the meaning of our lives on the Earth and begin to realize it as quickly as possible.

Therefore we have to regard both good and bad destinies as a boon. It becomes more understandable if we start to regard ourselves in all situations — as the disciples of God, Who sends us to the Earth for learning. And He is not going to give up teaching those who display their perspectiveness to Him, until they become worthy of merging with Him and enriching Him in this way!

It is with this purpose that our Creator creates material worlds and sends souls into them — so that these souls develop and evolve. It is in this way that the process of the Evolution of the Universal Consciousness goes on!

But in order to flow into the Creator, we have to cognize God in all of His Aspects: as the Creator, as the Holy Spirits, and as the Absolute.

However, while one remains a jiva (incarnate or non-incarnate), one cannot fulfill this task in fullness. Being jivas, we can only prepare ourselves for higher stages of development and to beginning the cognition of God. How do we do this? — by developing in ourselves all the aforementioned positive qualities and by getting rid of negative qualities. This task can be solved more easily with the help of the methods of psychical self-regulation, which are a part of knowledge called Raja Yoga. After all, we have to achieve, among other things, energetical purity of the organism and good health: while the body is contaminated with coarse energies, one cannot develop in the subtle and subtlest spatial dimensions. And the Creator, That we have to cognize, is the most subtle component of the Absolute!

Preparing ourselves for the higher stages of self-development — to Buddhi Yoga — we have to make anahata the dominant chakra. It is this chakra that is responsible for producing the emotions of love! And nothing but these emotions allow us to refine ourselves!

Emotions are the states of us (as consciousnesses). And we have to master the subtle and subtlest emotional states, have to become used to living in them!

Moreover, they are the emotions of love which allow the soul to become capable of MERGENCE! We learn this first by loving people and other manifestations of life in the Creation. Then we can direct our developed capability of loving — towards the Creator.

... And what is buddhi?

Contrary to the jiva, the buddhi is the part of the consciousness that is formed and further developed — with the help of the methods of Buddhi Yoga — in the subtle and subtlest spatial dimensions outside one's material body.

Development of the buddhi is ensured by direct growth of the spiritual heart, which is formed — in the beginning — on the basis of the anahata chakra. (One may describe it also as growth, expansion of the anahata chakra outside of the material body).

So let the spiritual heart grow to sizes of meters, kilometers, and even more!...

Then one has to supplement the developed anahata with the other chakras developed to the necessary degree. In this way one forms the structure called *dharmakaya* — "body of the Path". The term *dharmakaya* denotes one of the higher stages of development of the buddhi (which is followed by several other important stages of self-development on the spiritual Path).

Developing ourselves as dharmakayas, we gain even higher independence from the material bodies during incarnate lives. We become less susceptible to illnesses and other harmful factors. Also the power of the consciousness grows, which depends on the size of the consciousness and its ability to move outside the body. We learn to think without the use of the body, also to heal the body by influencing it from outside. But the most important thing is that it becomes easier for us to communicate with our Teachers — the Holy Spirits. And this is one of the important conditions for development of wisdom and for further self-improvement.

He who has achieved the fullness of Perfection as a buddhi — merges with the Primordial Consciousness (the Creator); such a Perfect One can be called a Buddha[9].

Yet there is an even more attractive stage of development: when the Perfect Buddhi, merged with the Primordial Consciousness, completely substitutes the jiva incarnated in the material body...

* * *

Many people live without thinking about why they live. They live with primitive egocentric attractions and reflexes: they seek pleasures, seek satisfaction of their greed and aggression...

The surrogate purposes, suggested to the members of the dominant religious movements, involve how to avoid hell and go to paradise through participation in rituals, through begging forgiveness from God for committed or non-committed sins, or even through killing infidels... But all aforementioned is not helpful from the evolutionary standpoint.[10]

God does not need anything like this — from us! He needs that we strive to become better, to become Perfect (Matt 5:48) — according to His Evolutionary Intention!

... What can I suggest for everyone to do? To study and to accept God's Intention, to find one's own place in the common Process of the Evolution of the Universal Consciousness — both in the aspect of mastering concrete methods of self-development and in the aspect of participating in this Great Process through one's own service to other people in the material world.

---

[9] Let me note that the words buddhi and Buddha have the same root.

[10] Another false way of "seeking spiritual self-realization" is the use of drugs, which do not contribute to one's spiritual advancement but destroy both the body and the consciousness.

Life filled with such everyday work, which is a manifestation of our love for God, is truly happy and blissful!

It is LIFE FOR GOD — life for Him rather than for myself!

Psychical Self-Regulation

In Europe, the ideas of psychical self-regulation originated namely in Germany. German physicians at the end of the 19th century began to develop the idea which they called *autogenic training*. The book *Autogenic Training* by Dr. Schultz became most well-known.

What was the subject of these recommendations? Relaxation, first of all. One could relax the body and the mind when lying on the back or sitting in the so-called "coachman's posture" (that is sitting on a chair in a stooped pose).

Of course, this had nothing in common with Yoga as a spiritual concept. But it played a positive role as a pre-history of psychical self-regulation.

The next large stage was the activity of Alexander Romen, a doctor-psychiatrist, who worked in Alma-Ata and in Moscow. The very term *psychical self-regulation* was invented by him. He dedicated much of his time and effort to this theme and published tens of works on this subject.

What did he write about? Mainly it was just propaganda of the idea: "Let workers of mines practice psychical self-regulation!", "Let workers of hospitals also...!", and so on...

It was very good, because thanks to him the term *psychical self-regulation* was accepted and became well-known. But Romen did not create any system of teaching psychical self-regulation.

Such a system was created for the first time by us, by our scientific-spiritual School. Why can I claim this?

Because efficient psychical self-regulation is not possible without the use of the functions of the chakras.

The chakras are reflexogenous zones of the emotional-volitional sphere. By moving the concentration of the consciousness into a certain chakra, we can — just thanks to this movement of the concentration — change the attunement of ourselves either to intellectual activity, or to the perception of the beauty, or to developing in ourselves the most significant quality — the capability for heart love, or to work activity, etc.

Without the use of the chakras, one cannot regulate one's own psychical state so efficiently.

It was our books that presented for the first time a description of the functions of the chakras and the methods for working with them. And for the first time, thanks to these books, the very concept of the chakras became legitimated in the USSR. Before this, the functionaries of the Communist Party, who supervised the science, asserted that the existence of chakras "was not proved by science" and therefore there were no chakras whatsoever! Thus the very subject of chakras was forbidden!

Yet chakras do exist. One can learn to use them — and this makes the beginning of the true path of yoga: Raja Yoga and the next higher stage — Buddhi Yoga.

I should also mention that there is a lot of different literature about chakras published by incompetent authors from different countries, and this literature has caused much harm.

For example, there is a statement (though this is not the most harmful one) that chakras contain structures resembling lotus flowers with different numbers of petals. But there are no lotuses in chakras! They do not contain such structures at all! Chakras are volumes filled with bioenergies or with the consciousness of man.

If one tries to see lotus flowers in the chakras, it is not harmful. By doing it, one learns to concentrate in the chakras.

Another error is extremely harmful: a long time ago another German author wrote a book where he claimed that the chakras have to be colored with different colors: since there are seven main colors of the rainbow, seven musical notes, seven chakras — all are seven — therefore every chakra has to have a corresponding musical note and a corresponding color. For example, it turned out that the anahata chakra has to be green...

And this tragic error caused a lot of harm to a very large number of people who sincerely wanted to become better and believed this false idea!

... Let us understand that it is in the anahata chakra that the spiritual heart has to be born and begin to grow. Then the spiritual heart has to transform — by its quality — to the state of the Holy Spirit and the Creator.

The Holy Spirit, the Creator — what is Their color? Tender-white-goldish! (Juan Matus spoke of an amber-tinted color).

And of what use is a green spiritual heart? God is not green at all! Who is green? Frogs... So with a green spiritual heart one can aspire to merge with swamp algae for example, but not with God!

All the chakras have to be made perfect. The most important of them is the anahata chakra. We can grow properly (as a consciousness) in qualitative and quantitative aspects only as spiritual hearts! There is no other possibility!

The state of all the chakras has to be made as close as possible to the state of God in the Aspect of the Creator. The most subtle stratum in the entire multidimensional Absolute is the Creator. We have to strive to submerge with the spiritual heart into Him; then we will be able to draw there all the other structures of our organisms that have value there.

What structures do I mean? There are the chakras (they were known in India in particular). There is also the concept of dantians (they were known to Chinese Taoists). The anahata chakra is the middle dantian. There is also the lower dantian — the power block of the organism consisting of the three lower chakras. And there are three upper chakras composing the upper dantian.

The main dantian is the middle one. And the other two are auxiliary. They are also necessary; they, too, have their own functions.

We can submerge into the Creator with all our dantians and merge with Him! This is an important goal which is worthy of every effort!

In order to be able to submerge all the dantians into the Creator, we have to bring them to His state. Let me repeat that His Light is tender-white-goldish. It makes no sense to try to enter the Creator with red, green, or other-colored chakras!

People who were engaged in the work of coloring their chakras — unless they wash out, which is very difficult to do, — they have no possibility to reach the higher stages on the Path of spiritual development! This is a trap! I ask everyone not to follow this harmful tendency and stay away from those who promote such vicious, dangerous pseudo-spiritual tendencies!

By the way, one may ask, pointing at me: "Why does he impose his opinion as if he alone is right? Why should others believe him?"

The point is that our group has managed to traverse the entire Path; we have reached the end of the Path. Of course, we know that there are possibilities for continuing work on ourselves, but we have traversed the entire Path — and therefore we can see very well the mistakes made by other seekers. If you have traversed and studied

the entire Path, if you know it — then you can see concrete stages of this Path and you can easily discern the
true and false attempts of other people who try to walk
this Path.

... So, we agreed that the main chakra is anahata.
And that the Straight Path is the Path of love for the
Creation and the Creator. And if through our love for the
Creation we have mastered the function of Love (with a
capital letter) — then we can fall in love with the Creator
too. Thanks to this love we merge with Him in the end.

If we have made at least initial steps on this Path
(namely, if we have developed ourselves as spiritual
hearts), then it is simple to develop further. Then we
learn to be subtler and larger spiritual hearts.

How can we grow? For this purpose we have to find
some forms that we can fill with ourselves (as spiritual
hearts). They can be "cocoons" of strong, powerful, subtle trees of different biological species. In our region,
they are poplars, pines, birches, spruces. I mean some particular plants which can be called *plants of power*; that
is, this concerns only certain specimens, not the entire
biological species.

So we can learn to fill their forms with ourselves as
the spiritual hearts by exiting from the anahata chakra
backward into these forms.

Then we can spread in expanses that we find in the
mountains, in the steppe, over the sea. By training in this
way, we become larger and larger spiritual hearts and
gain the ability to see with the consciousness.

Another important point is that the spiritual heart
necessarily has to have arms with hands; with these
hands we can support, nourish other living beings with
our power of love, help them.

If we go by this Path, then Holy Spirits very soon become visible for us. And if we are able to see Them, then

we can also hear Them: every one knows that it is more convenient to hear others if you see them.

By filling the forms of Consciousnesses of our Divine Teachers, the Holy Spirits, by attuning with Them — we grow with Their help up to the level when we can enter the Abode of the Creator.

Then one can look from the Primordial Consciousness at the Creation, one can come to the matter of one's own body — from another side, from the side of the Creator. And then one can transform the matter of the body...

... This is the Straight Path!

The idea of the Straight Path exists in Buddhism. It is also present in Islam — as a principle of directing one's attention toward the Creator.

The Straight Path is the shortest Path to full spiritual self-realization!

Of course, one has to keep in mind that the techniques of psychical self-regulation alone cannot enable one to grow to the fullness of the Perfection. Two other components are also necessary: intellectual and ethical ones.

We have to understand with the mind what is God; one needs to begin with this! But so few people can give a reasonable answer to this question! At best, they can tell you one of the names of God — and tell you that this is God. But they have no idea what is behind these names! They would not tell you that God is the Creator (the Primordial Consciousness), that God is also the Absolute (that is, Everything: the Creator together with His Creation)! And they do not know what we should do in relation to the fact that there is God!

The majority of people, who acknowledge the existence of God, begin to beg from Him salvation for themselves or, at best, for someone else as well. But in reality, God does not need our prayers or different variations of our worship per se! God needs our efforts on self-development!

Concerning repentance practiced in some spiritual movements, its purpose does not consist in begging forgiveness for our misdeeds; its purpose is to learn not to repeat mistakes!

If we have understood this, then the ethical component of spiritual development becomes actual for us; ethical work on oneself becomes meaningful. One does not have to kowtow all day long — but has to learn to avoid repeating mistakes!

But what is a mistake and what is not? We are able to discern this only if we understand what is God, what is man, what is the meaning of our lives! This meaning consists in our spiritual development! The meaning of life consists in spiritual development, not in accumulation of money or becoming elevated over others!

If we have understood this very well — only then can we make significant progress in our personal evolution in short periods of time.

Blessed Are the Pure in Heart!

In the Sermon on the Mount (Matt 5) there are several phrases of Jesus which are called *the Beatitudes*:

Blessed are the poor (i.e. those who have no possessions in the material world, who do not strive for material wealth) *in spirit* (more correct — by spirit, i.e. by one's own decision, by one's own will), *for theirs is the Kingdom of Heaven!*

Blessed are those who mourn (i.e. those remorseful for their misdeeds)[11], *for they will be comforted!*

---

[11] Yet, one should not do it too long: having learned — with the help of repentance — not to sin, we have to advance further on the spiritual Path in the state of positive emotions; otherwise we cannot succeed.

Blessed are the meek (i.e. those devoid of haughtiness and ambitiousness), *for they will inherit the earth!*

Blessed are those who hunger and thirst for righteousness[12], *for they will be filled!*

Blessed are the merciful, for they will obtain mercy!

Blessed are the pure in heart, for they will see God!

Blessed are the peacemakers, for they will be called Sons of God.

Blessed are those who are persecuted for righteousness' sake, for theirs is the Kingdom of Heaven!

Blessed are you when they revile and persecute you, and say all kinds of evil against you falsely for My sake! Rejoice and be glad, for great is your reward in the Heavens!

Now let us discuss one of these precepts, namely: "Blessed are the pure in heart, for they will see God!", because it is especially important for realization of the Teachings of God by us.

What did Jesus mean here? He said that God-the-Father and the Holy Spirit can be cognized and seen by people who have pure hearts.

* * *

What is *pure heart*?

And in general, how should one understand the term *heart* when it is used for speaking about spiritual growth?

Of course, it does not mean the anatomical material heart.

The opinion that the *heart* is an aggregate of all our instincts and emotions, including sexual attraction and passions, is also erroneous. The function of the spiritual heart is not related with sexual passions (strong egocentric, egoistic attractions) and even opposes them.

---

[12] I.e. whose greatest desires are to cognize and to fulfill what God requires.

There is another amorphous and inadequate use of the word *heart*: the mind (one of the examples — Acts 5:3).

It is very sad that these inadequate uses became widely accepted in literature, including religious literature, and even in some translations of the New Testament[13].

* * *

In order to understand what the *spiritual heart* is, we have to examine the bioenergetical structure of the human organism briefly (see [9] for more detail). It concerns the chakras, first of all.

---

[13] For example, in translation of the prayer-meditation Our Father (Lord's Prayer) it is not made clear that by "daily bread" Jesus meant not a material food but the higher spiritual knowledge, spiritual guidance which we should ask from God. This flaw resulted in masses of people (who consider themselves Christians) engaged in panhandling from God — instead of realizing His Teachings, which suggest that we strive for the spiritual Perfection (Matt 5:48).

Also the term "poor in spirit" does not mean feebleminded panhandlers-parasites, as it is usually interpreted, — but the spiritual warriors who have renounced seeking earthly wealth — for the sake of realization of the true meaning of life in accordance with the Teachings of God.

Also in the translation of the New Testament, there are the expressions "my (his, her) soul". This implies that man is a body in which some strange "soul" lives and this "soul" abandons man at the moment of death. Some people even develop opinions that one can "lose the soul", "steal the soul". But in reality, every man is an evolving soul, which enters a material body for a time in order to continue self-development. Therefore, one cannot "lose the soul"; one can only "lose the body"...

Also in the translation of the Epistles of Apostle Paul there are expressions that seem meaningless. There Paul described meditative methods taught by Jesus, but the translators could not understand them due to their incompetence...

(See also *The Original Teaching of Jesus Christ* in [8]).

43

Inside the chest of a human body, there is a bioenergetical organ called the *anahata chakra*. This chakra is responsible for providing bioenergies through a network of bioenergetical channels (meridians) to the lungs, to the anatomical heart, and to other organs located in the chest.

The anahata, as any other bioenergetical organ, is also a reflexogenic zone of the emotional-volitional sphere (more detail in [9]). It is the anahata that is responsible for generating the entire spectrum of the emotions of love. By moving the concentration of the consciousness into this chakra, one changes the state of the consciousness to the state of love.[14]

By working with moving the concentration of the consciousness between the chakras and main meridians, one can easily learn to change one's own emotional states and efficiency of work (both mental and physical one) at will and precisely. This is the basis of the system of psychical self-regulation, which was formed and described by us in our publications [9 and others].

In order to master the functions of the anahata, one has to start with cleansing it together with other chakras and main meridians — from dark bioenergetical contaminations. Then one has to expand the anahata inside the chest [9]. The anahata spread in this way occupies the volume of the chest from the collarbones to the beginning of the solar plexus.

Then one has to learn *to look with the eyes of the soul* from the anahata; and then — to habituate oneself to staying with the concentration of the consciousness in the anahata almost always: except for cases when one needs to act energetically in the material plane or to perform intensive intellectual work; in such cases one just needs to move the concentration of the consciousness into the chakra corresponding to the current situation.

---

[14] See also the chapter about Hesychasm in [9]; also [20].

The one, who has fully mastered this and has become firmly established in the anahatic state, achieves a paradisiacal life after the death of the body. This achievement can be lost only if one violates the ethical principles suggested to us by God.

Let me explain: the ethical components of the Teachings of God are aimed, first of all, at helping those, who are ready to follow these Teachings, to master the state of love and to become established in it.

For this purpose God suggests to us:

— renounce the capability to kill (except for cases of absolute necessity, such as attacks from mosquitoes, ticks, pathogenic microorganisms, etc.) other beings created by Him and embodied for their development into material bodies,

— do not do to others what we do not want to be done to ourselves,

— do not be haughty and arrogant,

— do not drink intoxicating drinks,

— do not be angry,

— do not be jealous,

— do not avenge,

— do not require back what was stolen from you...

And even give to the robber more than he wants to take from you, and to him who slapped you on one cheek turn another cheek also — but keep in these extreme situations the state of love! — and you will be in paradise then!

After all, paradise is the destiny of those who have realized the Teachings of God about love! And those who have accustomed themselves to coarse emotional states and rejected the Teachings of God — go to hell...

"God is Love" (1 John 4:8; 4:16). And — "Become closer to God!" (James 4:8). One can become closer to Him only by transforming oneself into Love. And it is possible to do — only through full realization of His precept which we discuss here.

Apostle James expressed the same idea in other words (James 4:8): "Purify your hearts!"

* * *

So, one can begin this path of transformation of oneself into Love with mastering one's own anahata chakra, including cleansing it of energetical contaminations which are caused first of all by one's own past ethical mistakes: by allowing oneself to enter coarse emotional states. One has to learn to live almost constantly in the anahatic state and never allow oneself to enter coarse states of the consciousness. In this way one gets rid of the "hardenedness" (Mark 6:52) of the potential germ of the spiritual heart.

Only after mastering everything said above, the development of the spiritual heart can begin. And then one can do more: one can begin developing oneself as a spiritual heart.

* * *

One of the features of the chakras is that the consciousness (soul), having settled in a certain chakra, can grow in size and enlarge this chakra, and then the consciousness can expand from this chakra.

It is very adverse if this happens with the chakras inclined to coarse states — manipura (the upper half of the abdomen including the solar plexus) and ajna (the middle of the head). People who allow this complex of chakras to become dominant are almost always irritated, angry, aggressive, hot tempered; their destiny is hell: "the outer darkness where there are weeping and gnashing of teeth" (Matt 8:12); these people oppose — by the quality of souls — God, Who is Love!

People of the anahatic psychotype are those who become closer to the state of God.

Moreover, if such people possess the necessary knowledge, they can significantly accelerate their further spiritual growth, mastering the next stages of the spiritual ascent.

After all, a soul can transform not only qualitatively but also quantitatively, that is to grow.

* * *

The spiritual heart is that part of the soul which in the beginning grows inside the cleansed anahata chakra if one realizes everything said above.

But then the spiritual heart can begin to grow intensively outside the material body.[15] And the possibilities of such growth are infinite! An aid in the realization of this task can be received from the ecopsychological methods described in our books [9 and others] and demonstrated in our films (see www.spiritual-art.info). With their help one can grow oneself — as a spiritual heart — to a size much larger than the size of our planet.

I should also note that a developed consciousness residing far outside the body possesses the fullness of thinking. And it can easily move in multidimensional space with the help of the arms of the consciousness, which grow from the spiritual heart and are coessential to it. (The same remains true after the death of the body). And one's closeness to the Primordial Consciousness and direct communication with the Holy Spirits increases the competency of such an adept in everything most important for incarnate people.

It is inside the spiritual heart developed so much, in its multidimensional depth, that the spiritual adept receives the possibility to easily explore the multidimensional structure of the Absolute and to come closer and

---

[15] This is mentioned by Apostle Paul, a disciple of Jesus Christ: "We... opened wide our hearts!" (2 Cor 6:11).

closer to the Abode of the Creator: the subtlest spatial dimension.

And then such an adept is accepted by the Creator into Himself — if he or she is worthy of it.

This is a brief description of the Path of full spiritual self-realization of man. You may find detailed information about how to go on this Path — in our books and films.

* * *

And let us remember: "Where your treasure is — there your heart will be also!" (Matt 6:21; Luke 12:34).

If we choose the Creator as our Treasure and aspire to cognition of Him and Mergence with Him in the Embrace of His Love — then we may find our Abode in Him.

But if our treasure is something earthly — then we will remain with this earthly.

And some people choose hellish entertainments as their treasure...

But God suggests: "Love your God with all your heart!" (Luke 10:27; Mark 12:30).

And it is up to us to choose our way: the Creator granted to us the freedom of will. He watches every one of us and forms our destinies, which are then realized by the Holy Spirits.

* * *

"Be perfect as your Heavenly Father is perfect!" — taught Jesus Christ (Matt 5:48).

How? — Jesus also gave the answer to this question: "Learn from Me!" (Matt 11:29). Learn — through the words said by Me and written down by My Disciples, learn by studying My Divine Essence, by aspiring to become like Me, also by accepting the Holy Spirits as your Guides

Who will teach you the same things that I taught and teach now (John 14:26; 15:26; Mark 3:29).[16]

And today Jesus is willing to help and helps everyone who walks the Path shown by Him![17]

What Is Truth?

This question implies a serious philosophical answer about the most important things in our existence: what is the essence of the Universe, what is the meaning of our lives on the Earth, and what is the best way to fulfill this meaning?

The most laconic answer is the following:

There is an ongoing Evolution in the Universal Organism of the Absolute. And every one of us should "blend" with this process most harmoniously.

For this purpose we need:

— To become sufficiently large, mobile, and strong consciousnesses (souls) — so as to gain the ability to move from one spatial dimension to another along the entire multidimensional scale, to personally cognize this multidimensional structure of the Absolute — from the boundary of hell — to the Abode of the Creator.

— To learn to firmly reside in the highest spatial dimension: in the Abode of the Creator — in Mergence with Him.

— To habituate ourselves to the state of Mergence, Coessentiality with the Creator, and then to develop the ability to be one with the entire Absolute.

From these highest states one can participate in the Evolutionary Process most successfully, on the Highest

---

[16] See [8].
[17] See [8].

Level of competence; in particular, one can help incarnate people in their spiritual development.

After disincarnation, such Perfect Individualities become Holy Spirits. And if They incarnate again on Their own Will among people — They become Divine Messiahs, Avatars.

However, even those, who have not yet achieved the highest stages of spiritual advancement, can find good work for themselves on the Earth — not only in personal development but also in service, which consists in participation in the Evolutionary Process.

And let everyone think: how can I serve others, how can I be useful to them?

Even taking care of plants and animals, providing other people with food, clothing, dwelling, giving birth to children and upbringing them, etc. — all this is also necessary. There are many other possibilities as well. And let the main principle of making choices here be the following:

To help everyone in everything good and to try to harm no one when possible: by deeds, words, and even by thoughts or emotions!

* * *

And now let us talk about this in more detail. Even among religiously thinking people, it is hard to find those who understand the meaning of the word *Absolute*. And there are very few who know the mechanisms of correct growth of the consciousness, or how to move from one spatial dimension to another and about cognition of the Creator in His Abode!

We discussed these questions many times in our books and films-lectures (see a list of the most important of them in the end of this book and on the site www. spiritual-art.info); here I am going to describe it briefly.

So, what is God?

This word means, first of all, the Creator (He is also called God-the-Father, Jehovah, Allah, Ishvara, Tao, Primordial Consciousness, Adibuddha, Svarog, and by other names in different languages). The Creator is not an old man sitting on a cloud, as He is depicted sometimes, but the infinite in size and time Ocean of the Subtlest Primordial Consciousness abiding in the highest spatial dimension.

By the word *God*, people also call the Representatives of the Creator coessential to Him — incarnate and non-incarnate. Such non-incarnate Representatives of the Creator are called the Holy Spirits; in the aggregate sense, They are called the Holy Spirit (that is, this term has a so-called collective meaning).

It is important to understand that the Creator and His Creation compose One Multidimensional Universal Organism. This is the Absolute, that is *Absolutely Everything*.

The Absolute exists in a state of constant, unceasing development, Evolution. It is for the sake of this process that the Creator creates islets of matter — planets where units of consciousness (individual souls) evolve through consecutive incarnations into material bodies of plants, animals, and people. The ultimate goal of their development is to achieve (through human incarnations) the Perfection and Mergence with the Creator.

From the above said it must be clear that man is not a body, contrary to what many people believe. Man is a soul, consciousness that is embodied only for a time into material bodies for the sake of going through the next stage of the development.

Every one of us possesses *freedom of will* — our right to make decisions in many small or large life situations, which affects our further destinies. (That is we build our destinies ourselves. And the Holy Spirits — our Divine Tutors and Teachers — realize these destinies.)

The process of destiny formation — which depends on ethically important decisions made by us — has to be studied by the branch of science called *ethics*. *Ethics* should be regarded as an integral part of *ecology* — the science about relationships of an organism with its environment. And the latter includes not only the world of material objects but also non-material forms of life with all non-incarnate beings and God.

What has to be the goal of our aspirations and deeds on the Earth (apart from fulfilling the most basic needs of our lives and of our closest companions)?

It is clear that our bodies have to be healthy. For this purpose it is useful to have medical knowledge, in particular, to know hygienic rules; also from childhood one has to temper the organism, to develop strength, endurance. It is also important to adhere to the *killing-free (vegetarian) diet*: feeding on bodies of killed animals results in contamination of the organism with coarse bioenergies; it also contradicts the principle of LOVE given to us by God. (However, our killing-free diet has to be made rich with protein food: milk products, eggs, mushrooms, nuts, etc. More detail see in [9]).

It is also very important to understand that one cannot achieve significant success on the spiritual Path without a developed intellect. People who have no developed intellect are not capable of comprehending what we discuss here! Even if they become believers, their religiosity — if they do not come from the beginning to a sound religious environment — is reduced to worshiping material objects (various idols, etc.), to mystical fear of warlocks, vampires, the end of the world; this leads to schizophrenia, to the coarsening of the consciousness, and — as a result — to hell...

... One can advance towards the Creator only through the refinement of the consciousness and development of love in oneself. Only developed love directed to the Creator can help one approach and merge with Him!

Therefore it is very important to ensure that children receive good education and that, as they grow up, the process of their intellectual development does not stop! Let the task of choosing a profession and working place also help them in this!

It is useful for every person to strive to comprehend the principles of righteous life on the Earth that are suggested to us by God more deeply. The main one of them is the principle of LOVE.

One cannot achieve ethical perfection without working with the reflexogenic zones of the emotional-volitional sphere — the chakras and some main meridians.

God is Love — He said these words for us. Yet it is wrong to understand this statement as "God will forgive all our sins". No. This statement means that we can realize our aspiration to the Creator, aspiration to the Mergence with Him — only through striving to become similar to Him, striving to become LOVE!

LOVE is an aggregate of corresponding emotional states. And it is desirable that every one of us habituate oneself to living in these states. As for coarse states of the consciousness, which program us to hell, — let them become so foreign to us that in no case can we enter them! Let me repeat that it becomes real for those who use the above mentioned system of training in psychical self-regulation [9]!

... So, let the anahata become the main chakra for us! It is in this chakra that the most important part of a human being — the spiritual heart — begins its growth. Let us learn to live in this chakra: to look, to listen, to perceive the outer world from it, to speak, to make decisions from this chakra!

In this way, we gradually become spiritual hearts — and then begin to grow outside the body. With time, in the process of this growth, we become spiritual hearts comparable in size to our planet and then even larger. The growing spiritual heart has to possess developed *arms of the consciousness* coessential to the spiritual heart. With the hands of these arms we can caress, stroke, heal...

The consciousness developed in this way accepts the function of thinking — outside of the material body.

Refusal of coarse emotional states and cultivation of the emotions of subtle tender love — together with the quantitative growth of oneself as a spiritual heart — this gives the ability to perceive (to see, to hear, to embrace) the Holy Spirits, Who become our real spiritual Teachers. Entering with the consciousness into Their giant Forms (Forms of Consciousnesses) allows one to begin mastering Mergence with Them. And then — They will lead Their deserving disciples into the Abode of the Creator.

* * *

Of course, one cannot achieve this quickly, immediately: the highest spiritual stages can be mastered only if one dedicates the whole life to God — to developing oneself for the sake of merging with Him and serving Him.

I also understand that some people can hardly believe that everything written here is real; it can happen to those who have not yet started serious work on perfecting themselves on the spiritual Path. However, by using the methods of self-development described in our books and demonstrated in our films one can make it real.

Let me note also that the knowledge presented here is not new. The same was taught (though in other words) by Thoth-the-Atlantean, Hermes Trismegistus, Pythagoras, Krishna, Lao Tse, Gautama Buddha, Jesus Christ, Babaji from Haidakhan, Sathya Sai Baba, and other Great Teachers [8]. It has always been taught by God! In our works we just present an integration of this knowledge and a detailed description of how one can traverse the spiritual Path and come to the spiritual heights which were demonstrated many times by Messengers of the Creator.

In conclusion let me stress again that the main direction of self-development on this Path is the development of the spiritual heart. All serious spiritual achievements are gained only through this!

... This is, in brief, the description of the full spiritual self-realization of man, the straight and shortest Path to the Creator. Let us go by this Path — and soon our lives will be filled with the joy of communication with God in blissful calm, without diseases and other calamities and suffering!

Evolution of Consciousness

The boundless universal space in reality is not empty. In it there abides an infinite in size and eternal Being Which is called the Absolute.

How can one become acquainted with Him? How can one see Him?

It is impossible to see Him in full — with the eyes of the material body.

Yet one can see, hear, and even embrace Him with the emotions of higher love! One can flow into Him and merge with Him! One can really do all this with oneself as a consciousness (soul) that has been developed to the necessary degree!

Why can one not perceive the entire Absolute through the organs of sense of the material body? Because the Absolute consists of several "layers" which are called spatial dimensions, planes of the multidimensional space, eons, or lokas (the two latter words are of Greek and

Sanskrit origins correspondingly). An individual consciousness is capable of perceiving only those objects and phenomena which exist within the "layer" where this consciousness dwells.

The Absolute can be compared with a multi-layered pie. Yet every one of these "Layers" exists in its "storey" of the multidimensional universe. And in order to cognize every such "Layer" directly, one has to enter it. However, this is not always easy to do.

For an ordinary healthy person, it is only easy to perceive the material plane. But the material plane is just one of the seven "layers of the pie".

Apart from the material plane, there are also the layers of hell, paradise, cosmic "repositories" filled with "building material" for future souls and for material objects (correspondingly — protopurusha and protoprakriti).

What is the difference between these eons? They differ by the place which they occupy on the scales of *coarseness — subtlety* and *density — refinement*.

Every eon is separated from another by a well-perceivable membrane, which can be likened to a boundary between water and transparent oil contained in the same vessel.

For studying the multidimensional structure of the universe one can use the concept of vectors of multidimensional scales.

One of such vectors goes through the multidimensional space between hell — and the Abode of the Creator.

Another vector goes between the world of matter — and the Creator.

Hell — as a spatial dimension — is the place of aggregation of coarse, despising souls expelled outside the Absolute. Jesus called this place "the outer darkness where there is weeping, and wailing, and gnashing of teeth" (Matt 8:12). It is the "rubbish heap" of the Absolute.

The world of matter is the densest eon.

And the Creator (the Primordial Consciousness) is the main and subtlest form of consciousness existing within the Absolute; it is the *Heart of the Absolute*.

... Let me also tell you that in the past I tried hardly to arrange into a single chart all the eons which I had known by that time. I could not do it for a long time, because I observed and entered pairs of eons of similar density and subtlety. And how can one arrange them into one sequence on the scale mentioned above?

The solution was found when I managed to realize that, yes, on every "storey" there is a pair of eons. The eons of each pair are separated from one another by one common membrane which can be called the *Mirror*. On the back side (with respect to the perceiver) of the *Mirror* there are "behind-the-mirror" eons; on the front side there are the worlds of matter, of individual souls, and of the Holy Spirits Who control the development of those souls.[18]

In this way the chart for studying the structure of the Absolute was created and then published in some of our books ([1,9 and others]). This chart allows spiritual seekers to master the lokas of the Absolute one after another with the help of this "search map".

---

[18] I understand very well that for a person who has no personal experience of cognition of God it is very difficult to imagine this.

I can only add that every human already possesses this entire structure as a potential for self-development. It is as if attached to the human body. One just needs to fill it with oneself as a consciousness — with the help of appropriate meditative practices.

From the standpoint of this knowledge we can also understand the meaning of the Biblical statement (Gen. 1:26,27) about the likeness between man and God (God — in the aspect of the multidimensional Absolute).

It also should be pointed out that one can find on that chart not the lokas themselves, but the entrances to them.

Of course, the use of this chart is not the only way to direct cognition of the Creator. Another possibility is the case when a Divine Teacher leads His or Her disciple through His or Her Mahadouble into the Abode of the Creator [9]; in this case, the disciple studies the structure of the Absolute afterwards. But the use of this chart allows one to gain a significant "margin of safety" for making further spiritual efforts.

Let me also note that if one has achieved in a certain way cognition of the Creator and has mastered the ability to enter the state of Mergence with Him, it does not signify the end of the Path. On the contrary, one receives new wonderful opportunities for further development.

* * *

Attainment of Mergence with the Creator was preached as the meaning and goal of our lives on the Earth by Thoth-the-Atlantean (Hermes Trismegistus), Pythagoras, Krishna, Jesus Christ, Gautama Buddha, also by Messiahs of our days — Sathya Sai Baba and Babaji from Hidakhan [2,5,8,10,13]. But the religious-philosophical ignorance of human masses instilled in them by various sects results in the fact that so many people do not understand why they appeared on the Earth and wander on the paths of suicide, drug addiction, criminality, and hatred toward everyone and everything...

... One may ask a question: "What do I need to do to achieve this goal?"

To answer this question, we first have to discuss the process of development of souls.

The most important thing to understand now is that the Absolute exists in the state of unceasing development, evolution.

This process goes on through the creation of individual particles of energy (purusha) that, having been incarnated into material bodies, grow gradually and become more and more complex and perfect — in order to eventually achieve that level of Perfection which would allow them to become worthy of flowing into the Primordial Consciousness and thus enriching It with themselves.

It is for this purpose that islands of the matter — stars and planets — are created in various parts of the universe. And then on planets suitable for this purpose, there begins development of organic bodies and incarnation of germs of souls into these bodies.

Thus two parallel evolutionary processes guided by God begin: evolution of organic bodies and evolution of souls incarnated in these bodies.

Souls get incarnated into material bodies of increasing complexity many times and thus go through the stages of vegetal, animal, and then human life.

And the task of us, humans, consists in conscious and active development with the purpose of achieving Divinity and merging into the Primordial Consciousness, and then continuing to live in It as Its Integral Parts and to act from It helping other evolving beings.

… So, having understood the meaning of our lives on the Earth, it would be appropriate to discuss now how one can realize it most successfully.

* * *

Every intellectually developed incarnate person can notice the vast diversity of people around. This concerns not the difference of the bodily features: sex, ethnicity, color of the skin and hair, etc. — all these do not matter! Another difference is more important — the difference of qualities between souls.

There are two main factors which define the quality of the soul and its corresponding capabilities in the task of spiritual development at present. They are: a) the soul's psychogenetic age[19] and b) what qualities were developed by this person during the last stages of his or her personal evolution. These qualities can be positive or negative; in other words, they can be contributing to the evolutionary progress of the soul or impeding this progress.

But how can one discriminate between vicious and virtuous qualities of the soul? Is there an objective criterion for such discrimination?

For example, for many alcoholics it would be the following: if you do not want to drink with me, then you do not respect me, then you are my enemy! And if you drink with me, then we are friends with you forever!

In some religious sects they believed and believe now that it is a feat to kill infidels. The more infidels you kill, the more chances to go to paradise you have!

There are many despising examples of this kind. They concern national and sexual prejudices, rules of how one should or should not dress, etc.

Such morals dominate among the masses of ethically perverted souls, who live in constant search of objects for their hatred... They involve into their movements other souls, who are younger and therefore submissive, and lead them, too, to hell...

But God always suggests to incarnate people the opposite thing: to love, to give, to be tender and caring toward each other, not to judge, not to hate, to forgive... [2,5,8,9,13,19-20,23-30]

One may ask: why? After all, if we rid the Earth of all those... — then it would be more joyful and easy for all to live! And God finally would be able to come to us and make us happy!...

But God has a different opinion.

---

[19] The age of the soul, in contrast to the age of the body.

He Himself says that He is Love (1 John 4:8) and suggests that we learn this from Him (Matt 11:29). In order to become closer to Him, one has to make efforts on changing oneself qualitatively, thus approaching Him — the standard of Perfection! (James 4:8)

He also is Calm and ultimate Subtlety. He suggests that we learn these qualities from Him as well [8-13,24-30].

Besides, He tells us about the Wholeness of the Absolute, suggests that we flow into this Wholeness and live in such states of the consciousness that habituate us to the state of unity and mergence with Him rather than separateness.

After all, can we come to Mergence with Him if we are used to saying "no" to everyone?[20]

On the contrary, one has to learn to MERGE IN LOVE — in order to become able to merge with the Main Beloved!

The symbol of love and mergence is "yes" rather than "no".

And, in general, can we sincerely (not only in words) fall in love with the Creator if we have not yet learned to fall in love with people?

And can we expect responsive love and caress from the Creator if we are not capable of loving His Creation, are not careful toward nature in general and toward concrete incarnate beings: plants, animals, people?

* * *

God commanded to people DO NOT KILL (Exodus 20:13), do not use for food bodies of creatures which con-

---

[20] This statement does not mean however that we always have to say "yes" to vicious people. We have to develop the ability to distinguish: what leads us to God and what leads us to hell, i.e. to the separateness from God.

tain blood (Exodus 9:4; also [9]). Yet how many people follow these commandments? And violation of these commandments leads to burdening one's destiny with diseases and inability to progress on the Path to the Creator.

… Every one of us has to constantly think about what God wants me to be. Yes, one has to listen to what other people say about it, yet one also has to learn to see and to hear the Will of the Creator behind the opinions of people.

Let us think: why did Jesus suggest not to demand the things that were stolen from you, and even to give to the robber more than this person wants to take from you, and to the one who slapped you on one cheek turn the other cheek as well (Matt 5:39-42)? Jesus suggested it for us so that we learn not to exit the state of love whatever may happen! After all, every instance of leaving this state of consciousness makes us more distant from the Creator!

The development of the ability to attune with the beauty of nature and with the best works of art, the control over the emotional sphere, behavior and the entire way of life based on calm and benevolent attitude to all the living — both to incarnate and not incarnate — this can prepare us for the ascent to the summit of Perfection!

And then the principle stage on this ascent will be — to master the system of psychical self-regulation developed by us [9 and others].

This system includes, among other things, cleansing and development of the main energy structures of the organism (the chakras and meridians). One cannot attune with the Divine Subtlety of the Holy Spirits and the Creator if one's body is contaminated with coarse energies, which get accumulated, first of all, from coarse emotions and wrong nutrition.

Another important emphasis in this system of training has to be made on the development of the spiritual heart [1-15,19-20,29-30].

The spiritual heart is that part of the soul which may begin to develop in the anahata chakra located in the chest.

This chakra is the emotiogenic zone of the emotional-volitional system and it is responsible for producing the emotions of love. If one moves the concentration of the consciousness into this chakra, this will allow one to get rid of coarse states of the consciousness, to destroy pathogenic thinking dominants — and to come to pure, subtle states of love.

The consciousness can change not only qualitatively but can also grow quantitatively.

If one grows oneself in coarse states of the consciousness, then one will for sure become an inhabitant of hell.

If, on the contrary, we grow ourselves as spiritual hearts, we transform ourselves by becoming subtler and larger, by becoming giant spiritual hearts — and then we gain the ability to see the Holy Spirits and after this the Creator in His Abode, to converse with Them as easily as we converse with the people closest to us... We can even begin to try to embrace the infinite Creator by submerging our loving Arms of the Consciousness into Him and expanding them in Him — the Arms which grow from the giant Spiritual Heart... Then we can easily completely[21] submerge ourselves into Him, merge with Him, and become Him.

And what is next? — The next thing that we should do is to learn to act *from* Him. We can master this by learning from the Holy Spirits — from Those Who entered Him earlier.

---

[21] In this case, completely means "with all the best from other dantians". This can be mastered with the help of special methods.

* * *

Such a level of communication with the Primordial Consciousness and with Its Representatives allows Those Who have traversed this entire Path to evaluate all the variations of attempts of spiritual ascent made by other seekers of the Path and to help them avoid making mistakes[22]; also to directly impart to people the Will of the Creator, His Teachings.

However, I ask you not to make the mistake, that many people make, by believing that God will help them in their selfish intentions! God is not our servant! It is people who have to become servants of God!

The intention of the Creator towards people is that they develop correctly, grow spiritually. He is ready to talk to people almost exclusively on this subject. The examples of this are the methodology of the Straight Path of spiritual development given by Him and the biographies of the Holy Spirits — the Divine Teachers — narrated by Them [8]. From these autobiographical stories, one may become acquainted with many variations of mastering the Path to the Creator and can choose the most convenient one for oneself.

Selfish desires are incompatible with the spiritual Path, and in general they have no place in relationships with God! It is so because they separate man from God by opposing the human "I" to Him.

The one who has approached the Perfection serves with all one's strengths only God, and not oneself. This service implies self-sacrifice. It makes sense to sacrifice

---

[22] In particular, it is necessary to stress that all real achievements on the spiritual Path are gained without the use of narcotics. Meditative work has to be performed in the right mind and without harming the organs of the body such as the brain, liver, kidneys, etc.

to God one's own life — rather than the lives of others — contrary to what followers of primitive sects do.

And — having sacrificed the personal interests and the personal "I" — man flows into the great "I" of the Primordial One!

* * *

So, the most important thing on the spiritual Path is the development of the spiritual heart; it is useful and adequate for all people including children.

It is also necessary to study and to realize in life the ethical principles suggested for us by God. Yet in this matter there must be age differentiation. For example, if one begins to teach children "to turn the other cheek" unconditionally, this will reduce their chances to develop the power aspect of the soul, which is necessary to withstand the trials of the spiritual Path. One first has to learn to fight, to develop the willpower and self-discipline through this — and only then one can apply to oneself all the suggestions of God: they are intended for mature people!

Another thing: it is very important to develop the intellect in all possible ways. Without a developed intellect one cannot understand and realize in life the ethical principles suggested by God. And the developed intellect is even more important for understanding the multidimensional structure of the Absolute and for being able to explore and study it without danger for one's own psychical health.

One may say that the level of one's intellectual development defines what part of the spiritual Path that person can traverse during the foreseeable part of his or her life.

Not everyone is capable of traversing the entire Path quickly. Yet one has to do everything one can to achieve this goal. In particular, in this way we create positive karma (destiny) for ourselves — and make our lives more joyful and happy! Besides, the more we traverse now, the lesser part of the Path will remain for us to traverse in the future!

The "Third Eye" and the "Sun of God"

The ideas about the potential existence of the "third eye", which can be opened with the help of special methods in order to gain clairvoyance, appeared most likely thanks to an ancient saying of Krishna recorded in the Bhagavad Gita [8,11]:

8:9. The one who knows everything about the Eternal Omnipresent Ruler of the world, the One subtler than the subtlest, the Foundation of everything, formless, shining like the Sun behind the darkness,

8:10. who at the moment of departure does not distract the mind and love, being in Yoga (In Mergence with Ishvara — with God-the-Father, the Creator, the Primordial Consciousness), who OPENS THE PASSAGE OF ENERGY BETWEEN THE EYEBROWS — such one attains the Highest Divine Spirit!

8:11. This Path which men of knowledge call the Path to the Eternal, which spiritual warriors go through self-control and liberation from passions, which brahmacharyas walk — that Path I will describe to you in brief.

8:12. Having closed all gates of the body (i.e. the organs of sense), locked the mind in the heart, directing the Atman to the Supreme, being established firmly in Yoga,

8:13. chanting the mantra of Brahman AUM and being conscious about Me — anyone departing so from the body attains the Supreme Goal.

Later on, many people striving to develop clairvoyance, but not understanding the essence of the Teachings of God, dedicated themselves to self-harming by concentrating in the point between the eyebrows... This resulted in activation of the ajna chakra — one of the coarsest chakras. And this, in its turn, resulted in the development of a "sharp", "piercing" unpleasant look in such persons and in coarsening of the entire consciousnesses... Moreover, the ajna chakra (by the way, its name is translated as "non-wise" or "foolish", simply speaking) is the center of the human lower self! Therefore, concentration in it provokes accelerated growth of egocentrism — as opposed to the necessity of realization of God-centrism on the spiritual Path... Thus such people moved in the direction opposite from Perfection...

But one has to walk to Perfection with the help of completely different methods! They imply development of oneself as a spiritual heart, as love! Krishna and all other Divine Teachers told us about this (see [8])!

By the way, even from this short excerpt from the Bhagavad Gita we can see that one has to begin spiritual efforts not with concentration in the head chakra.

Let us see what Krishna talks about in this excerpt:

a) one has to cognize everything about Ishvara, Who is the subtlest form of consciousness of all existing in the universe;

b) one has to learn to see Him in the form of a *Divine Sun*, in particular;

c) one has to learn to live with the concentration of the consciousness in the Atman;

d) one has to stay in Mergence with Ishvara;

e) one has to learn to live with the mind functioning not in the head of the material body but in the developed spiritual heart (which begins its growth from within the purified and developed anahata chakra);

f) one has to be free from subjection to earthly passions.

Let me repeat that mere concentration of the unrefined and coarse consciousness in the ajna chakra leads to an increase in the coarseness of the entire consciousness (soul) and to growth of egocentrism. The way to cognition of Ishvara is opposite and consists, first of all, in development of oneself as love and subtlety! Without development of these two qualities in oneself, one cannot cognize God and come to Mergence with Him! And one cannot achieve these qualities without zealous work on full purification and principal increase of the spiritual heart (more detail in [9 and others]).

One has to work with the ajna chakra as well, but with the help of other methods: not by concentrating in it and not by trying to look through the point between the eyebrows.

By the way, what is this point? It is the center of the "window" of the ajna chakra. This "window" includes the forehead, the eyes, and the region of the nose. Yes, this "window" has to be opened and cleansed — together with the chakra. (One has to do it also with all other chakras and their "windows").

How can one do it? The basic practical methods are described in book [9]. At the final stage, this work is performed with the use of the *Fire* of the *Divine Sun* ("Sun of God").

The "Sun of God", according to Jesus Christ [17], is a visible (to the eyes of a soul developed as a spiritual heart) structure exceeding in size by thousands of times the usual disk of the Sun that we see in the sky.

The "Sun of God" appears in a place where any of the Greatest Divine Teachers, such as Krishna, Jesus, Sathya Sai Baba, Surya, Lada, Yamamata, Eagle, Adler, and Others (see [8]), comes out from the Abode of Ishvara into the world of the Creation.

In order to purify the ajna chakra and its "window", one has to learn to see the "Sun of God", to enter It with the consciousness, to merge with It, to come with Its *Fire* to the material body, to enter the anahata chakra from behind, to rise through the middle meridian up to the ajna chakra— and then to emanate forward from it as a flow of the Divine *Fire*.

How can one learn it? The only possibility is to follow the principal methodological steps described in book [9].

What is the result of this work? In addition to full elimination of all defects in the body treated with this *Fire*, it ensures complete purity of thinking.

Further treatment of the entire body with the Divine *Fire* can result in transfiguration of the energy composing the matter of the body and can provide one with the ability to control the matter of the body and the matter of other objects.

* * *

So, does moving the *Fire* through the ajna chakra constitute "opening of the 'third eye'"? No!

The point is that the true "third eye" originally resides not in the ajna chakra but in another chakra — in the anahata!

If one develops oneself as a spiritual heart, then such a soul gains an organ of vision capable of seeing in the subtlest spatial dimensions (lokas, eons). That is, such a spiritual seeker becomes capable of seeing the Holy Spirits (Who compose Brahman) and Ishvara in His Abode. In this case, God — in His different Manifestations — can be seen as clearly as we see material objects with the eyes of our material bodies!

And then such a seeker can create the Divine *Fire* by coming out from the Abode of Ishvara and can try to burn away with this *Fire* everything in the body that looks denser than the Divine *Fire*. Then not only the consciousness (soul) becomes Divine but the body as well.

This is, by the way, the *Fire from Within* that Juan Matus (Don Juan) described to Carlos Castaneda [16].

And let me repeat that one has to begin with developing oneself as a spiritual heart, which is the organ of love that enables us to learn to truly love the Creation and then the Creator as well.

Krishna said the following about this:

11:54. ... Only love can contemplate Me in My innermost Essence and merge with Me!

13:10-11. Steadfast and pure love for Me... — this is acknowledged as true.

12:14. ... Seeking Unity with Me, resolutely cognizing the Atman, devoted the mind and consciousness to Me — such a loving Me disciple is dear to Me.

12:20. ... All... for whom I am the Supreme Goal — ... are dear to Me above all!

Well, it is such "third eyes" that we have to strive to gain! Isn't it?

Dharma, Dharmakaya, Nirodhi, Nirvana

The term *dharma* has two similar meanings: *the law of existence* and *predestination*.

One can talk about dharma as about individual predestination of a particular person or as about the Universal Law of the Evolution and of our existence (Sanathana Dharma, in Sanskrit).

It is clear that an individual dharma can be understood fully only on the basis of understanding the universal dharma. Therefore, let us now examine the basic knowledge about the Sanathana Dharma.

In the boundless universal space there exists One Macrobeing called the Absolute.

It is eternal and infinite in size.

It is multidimensional, i.e. It exists simultaneously in several spatial dimensions called lokas in Sanskrit or eons in Greek.

Its main Essence is the Primordial Consciousness, Which is called — in different languages — by the terms Ishvara, the Creator, Allah, Tao, God-the-Father, etc. The Primordial Consciousness is the Heart of the Absolute, i.e. the Main Part of the Absolute. It exists in the highest, subtlest spatial dimension, which is called the Abode of the Creator.

The Absolute exists in an unceasing process of Its further development, evolution.

It is with this purpose that the Creator creates islets of the material world (prakriti) of protomatter (proto-prakriti). Then germs of future souls get embodied on these islets of matter with the purpose of development. They go through stages of growth in material bodies of different biological species by incarnating first in small bodies of the most primitive structure, then in vegetal and animal bodies — up to incarnations into human bodies.

The meaning of this process is to allow individual souls to develop up to the level when they become worthy of infusing into the Primordial Consciousness and thus enriching It with themselves. It is clear that such a goal can be realized only after many successful human incarnations.

The Primordial Consciousness is an Aggregate of all the Souls Who have merged with It. This process of enriching of the Primordial Consciousness goes on forever. It takes place now as well.[23]

---

[23] One can read about this in the Gospel of Apostle Philip, Who was a personal Disciple of Jesus Christ [8].

Let us note that on each planet inhabited by incarnate beings, two evolutionary processes take place: a) evolution of organic bodies which are used for incarnations of souls, and b) evolution of souls which are embodied into those bodies. Both these processes are controlled by the Primordial Consciousness — through the Holy Spirits.

The speed of evolution at the human stage of development depends to a significant degree on the person himself or herself. Every one of us has the freedom of will in choosing one's own path: to the Perfection in the Mergence with the Primordial Consciousness — or in the opposite direction, to hell: to the "rubbish heap" of the Evolutionary Process.

What can we do to participate most successfully in this Evolutionary Process?

One may ask this question in another way to make the answer more evident: how can we become Perfect, what are the components of the Perfection?

Let us see: what are the qualities of the Primordial Consciousness (as the Standard of Perfection)?

It is the most subtle (as opposed to coarseness) form of consciousness, and It is giant!

Therefore, we have to begin with accustoming ourselves to living in the subtle and subtlest emotional states. Let us remember that emotions are the states of ourselves as individual consciousnesses (souls)!

If we accustom ourselves to subtle emotions, we will appear after the death of the bodies among other souls like us, in paradise at least.

If we accustom ourselves to staying in emotional coarseness, we program ourselves for life in hell among other beings like us.

But our ultimate goal is to settle in the Abode of the Primordial Consciousness in the infinite Embrace of Mergence with other Holy Spirits. Thus we enrich the Primordial Consciousness with all the best accumulated by us in ourselves and gain an opportunity to serve other evolving beings from the position of our own Highest Perfection.

In order to help us in mastering subtlety of the consciousness, Representatives of the Creator imparted to us corresponding principles of life, precepts. They contain, among other things, recommendations to learn to live without negative emotions. The most complete sets of such precepts were given to us through Jesus Christ and Sathya Sai Baba. Let me also note that mastering these principles of life is not possible without mastering the art of psychical self-regulation [9].[24]

One also has to understand that a crucial factor on the Path to Perfection is the level of one's intellectual development. Without a developed intellect, one can neither comprehend the essence of the Universal Evolutionary Process nor understand the meaning of concrete Divine precepts!

Thus we can understand the reason for numerous religious perversions, which are dominant on our planet today. They include deification, imposition of various religious "rules" on believers: which clothes one has to wear, which prayers to recite, which bodily movements to perform, etc. And quite often, it substitutes for the true spiritual efforts on self-development!

Intellectual development is the aspect of perfection which goes on most slowly as compared to the other aspects. And we have to understand that one should not teach serious techniques of the development of the consciousness to intellectually undeveloped people. This concerns, first of all, people who are young — both ontogenetically (i.e. in the current incarnation) and psycho-

---

[24] These subjects are also covered in our educational films. See www.spiritual-art.info.

genetically (i.e. from the standpoint of the evolutionary age of the soul) [5-11].

One of the parameters for appraising one's intellectual abilities is the creativeness of the mind.

What should one do to develop the intellect most efficiently? The answer is simple: to study everything that is useful for moving on the spiritual Path. This includes knowledge on medicine, biology, philosophy, ethnography, different kinds of art, geology, physics, etc.

* * *

Dharmakaya is "a body of the Path". It does not concern our ordinary physical bodies. The point here is that we have to grow with our new non-material bodies of energies of individual consciousnesses — so that in these bodies we can traverse the Path from the state of an ordinary person to spiritual Perfection and to Mergence with the Primordial Consciousness.

Soul (in the usual meaning of the word) is denoted in Sanskrit by the term *jiva*.

Yet in Sanskrit there is another word: *buddhi*. It denotes a soul developing with the help of the methods of Buddhi Yoga. The term *Buddha* has the same root as the word *buddhi*. Buddha is the One Who has achieved Perfection through Buddhi Yoga.

By the way, Krishna in the Bhagavad Gita [8,11] conveys information about Buddhi Yoga among other things.

It may be said that Buddhi Yoga is a system of methods for the development of dharmakayas. The word *dharmakaya* is a synonym of the word *buddhi* (it can be a full or partial synonym — depending on the meaning assigned to this word in different spiritual schools).

What is the methodology of Buddhi Yoga?

The initial basis of this methodology consists in development of the *spiritual heart* — an energy structure that is initially formed in the anahata chakra; then it has to be developed and to begin functioning outside the material body.

It is important to note that everyone — regardless of the age of the body or soul — can prepare him/herself for mastering this large stage of self-development and benefit much from this. Namely, it implies "opening" and purifying the anahata, learning to live in it and to perceive the outer world from it, to react to outer information — from it. It is important because this chakra is responsible for producing the entire spectrum of the emotions of love. Everyone can become convinced of this: no coarse emotions (like irritation and other forms of anger) can occur while we stay with the consciousness in the anahata! While being in the anahata we can experience only the emotions of love: tender and caring attitude, gratitude, admiration, respect, etc.

Those who have mastered thus the art of psychical self-regulation can avoid many misdeeds and wrong thoughts that originate from one's own coarse emotional states and result in ill karmic consequences.

Those who have achieved stable anahatic states of the consciousness, even if they do not manage to achieve Mergence with the Primordial Consciousness in the current incarnation, — become inhabitants of paradise until the next incarnation. And the next incarnation will be very favorable for them in all respects, including conditions for continuing spiritual development.

... How can we develop the dharmakayas?

On this path we have to learn:

1. To enter the anahata with the entire consciousness and to look from within it to all six directions with an emphasis on looking backward.

2. To expand the spiritual heart outside the body; helpful in this regard are the methods of filling with oneself (as a consciousness) the *cocoons* of trees suitable

for this work, filling expanses over large water bodies, over sand deserts, or in the mountains. After that, if the practitioners have achieved the necessary level of refinement of the consciousness, they can begin to master Mergence with the Holy Spirits in Their Mahadoubles; training in filling with oneself the expanses found in the lokas of protoprakriti and protopurusha is also very important [9]; the mechanism of Mergence with Brahmanic Manifestations of the Primordial Consciousness (i.e. with the Holy Spirits) is based on the ability to make the lower self disappear and to replace it with "non-I" (it is described in the next part of this chapter).

3. To connect all the best that was accumulated in the other dantians, including the intellectual and power potentials, to the spiritual heart; for this purpose, at a certain stage of formation of the dharmakaya, one pays attention to constructing it of the chakras that are moved outside the body; in the beginning of this process the dharmakaya is made as a "pillar" of interconnected chakras, the upper four of them remain partially in the body and the lower three chakras extend this "pillar" backward-downward with respect to the body; all this is done on a scale much larger than the body: these chakras have to become giant; a developed dharmakaya is a structure that has a size of many kilometers (and it is clear that one cannot grow up to such a size quickly: one needs years of making efforts); the valuable structures of the upper dantian are moved to the dharmakaya in another way[25].

4. To act effectively with the arms and hands of the dharmakaya; this is important for moving in multidimensional space and for exerting transformational influence on one's own body and on other objects;

---

[25] We discuss this subject in more detail in the film Kundalini Yoga.

5. To live and to act in the state of one's own Mahadouble far outside the material body.

6. It is desirable to create not one but two dharmakayas: left and right ones; it is useful for cognition of Paramatman.

Further efforts have to be directed at achieving Mergence with the Primordial Consciousness and strengthening this Mergence also at helping other worthy people on this Path.

* * *

Mastering *Nirodhi* implies "burning away", destruction of one's own lower self for the sake of Mergence with the Higher I: with the Atman and then with Paramatman, Which exist in the higher spatial dimensions.

Without cognizing Nirodhi one cannot achieve Higher Nirvana, which consists in stable Mergence with the Primordial Consciousness.

Such a Mergence implies that an individual human consciousness flows into the infinite Universal Ocean of the Primordial Consciousness. To merge with this Consciousness means to sink and to disappear in It![26] Only in this way one can become It!

For this purpose one has to learn to disappear as a self and to enter the state of non-I. Thus the individual consciousness of the practitioner enters the state of full mergence with the Consciousness existing around the practitioner. The method of achieving this is called *total reciprocity*.[27]

---

[26] Only after becoming established in such a Mergence, one can then restore the Individuality (now Divine) by coming out from the Primordial Consciousness and yet remaining firmly merged with It by the main Part of Oneself.

[27] It is demonstrated in our film Advaita Yoga.

One has to learn it first in one of the subtle lokas — then one becomes able to master it in the loka of the Primordial Consciousness.

It is important to note that the above said can only be cognized with the structures of an individual consciousness based on the developed spiritual heart. There are no other possibilities.

Preparatory elements of self-development that allow one to master Nirodhi are the basic norms of ethically correct behavior suggested to us by Representatives of the Primordial Consciousness. They suggest that we strive to rid ourselves of numerous manifestations of egocentrism such as envy, jealousy, the capability to feel offended, to revenge, to display conceit or any other variations of self-elevation and self-praise. Let me note that all the mentioned emotional states can occur only in the head chakra ajna and can never be in anahata.

The developed *lowliness of mind* (lowly feeling of oneself with regards to different variations of education for myself by my Main Teacher — the Primordial Consciousness) together with *total reciprocity* allow one to master *Godcenteredness* (God-centrism) as opposed to human *egocentrism*. The center of self-perception of such an adept can be moved easily and naturally into the Heart of the Absolute; such an adept can really feel the entire Evolutionary Stream of development and advancement of consciousnesses within the Absolute! He or she flows into this Stream, merges with it, and feels oneself as it! Staying in this Stream allows the adept to fully realize the principle suggesting that we love other evolving beings as ourselves or even more than ourselves. Selfishness, envy, competitiveness — such emotions and thoughts can no longer occur! Now I am only an integral part of the Stream of the Evolution, and there can be no difference to me who will reach the Goal first; I help everyone as much as I can, including those who advance quicker than I!

* * *

The term *Nirvana* denotes the state of Mergence with a Divine Consciousness.

Krishna [8,11] talked about three kinds of such Mergence: a) Nirvana in Brahman (namely, Mergence with Holy Spirits in Their giant Forms — Mahadoubles), b) Nirvana in Ishvara (in the Primordial Consciousness, in the *Heart of the Absolute*), and c) Nirvana as Mergence with the entire Absolute.

One can also distinguish two Nirvanic states: static and dynamic.

One of the two manifestations of the latter is one's activity as a Mahadouble in helping embodied beings.

Another dynamic state is the Divine *Fire*.

The above said corresponds to two observable states of the Primordial Consciousness: a) Transparent Calm and b) Fiery state when the Primordial Consciousness enters the state of increased activity.

Those Who have cognized the higher forms of Nirvana can become convinced of the existence of this phenomenon from Their own experience: now They, too, can abide in the Blissful Calm of the Primordial Consciousness, in full Mergence in Love with Others Who have achieved this, — or They can enter the state of Divine *Fire* when performing certain kinds of activity.

The Fiery state of One Who has achieved Nirvana can be used for transforming the energy composing the matter of One's material body. As a result of such work, One gains the ability to take the body out of the world of matter and then to materialize it again whenever it is necessary. This ability was demonstrated by Jesus Christ; some other Divine Teachers also possessed this ability [8].

The Divine *Fire* does not burn the righteous. But it is frightening and painful for those who go to hell or have settled in hell already. This is the source of legends about sinners burning in fires of hell...

Meditation: Steps of Mastering (lecture)

Once, many years ago, I was invited to come to one of the classes of a spiritual group.

In the beginning, they talked about some organizational problems; then the leader announced that "now the most important part — meditation — begins"!

I waited with interest to its beginning. I waited... Ten or fifteen minutes passed in silence... Suddenly... he said that the meditation was over and that everyone could go home...

It turned out that these people understood meditation... as sitting on chairs in silence...

... There was another similar case. The parents of a six year old boy (they attended classes on Hatha Yoga) once entered their son's room and saw him sitting motionless on his bed with closed eyes and crossed legs.

They asked:

"What are you doing?"

"I am meditating!" — he replied.

His understanding of meditation was the same.

... Other people understand meditation just as careful thinking about a particular subject, for example about "Love", "God", etc...

In the same way the word *meditation* is interpreted in some dictionaries as an act of thinking deeply about something.

The task of today's conversation is to discuss this subject more seriously.

* * *

The term *meditation* can be defined as one's personal efforts on developing oneself (as a soul, consciousness) in the directions of correct functioning of the emotional sphere, refinement and quantitative growth of the consciousness, direct cognition of God in the Aspects of the Primordial Consciousness, of the Holy Spirit, of the Absolute, and attainment of Mergence with God.

* * *

The evolutionary development of each person consists of three main components, which are closely related with each other: intellectual, ethical, and psychoenergetical ones.

Meditation is the main means of realization of the third one of these components, first of all. But it can also significantly accelerate one's growth in the other two directions.

Now I want to draw your attention to a very important rule of spiritual work: meditative training must not go ahead of the ethical component of one's development and must not exceed one's intellectual capacity in the current incarnation!

In other words, aspiration of the student is not enough for initiation into higher meditations. One must also take into consideration, among other things, the student's ontogenetic age (i.e. the age in the current incarnation) and the psychogenetic age as well (i.e. the entire personal evolution of this soul).

Therefore, teachers and practitioners should be careful with what concerns the practice of meditation.

On the other hand, there are meditations which are absolutely safe to practice: they can bring nothing but benefits to everyone, including children. They are, for example, attunement to the harmony and beauty of nature, which is shown in our films and photo galleries; attunement to appropriate works of different kinds of art, including music, singing, dancing, etc.

It is important to understand that refining BEAUTY, development of the emotions of love, renunciation of all forms of coarseness — these are the first steps away from hell — to our Creator!

On the contrary, the destiny of those who develop coarse qualities is physical and mental illnesses and other kinds of suffering during life in the body. After the death of the body, they appear in the coarse spatial dimensions (eons, lokas) among other beings like them; this is what hell is.

It is most important for everyone to apply this information. And it is also important to convey this to people of all countries and confessions!

One's coming to hell or paradise is determined not by one's membership in a particular religious organization and not by one's actions, but by the qualities of the soul!

The destiny of those who have become accustomed to coarseness is hell.

The destiny of those who are loving, forgiving, tolerant, and refined is paradise.

And those who reach the level of refinement of the Creator can cognize Him and merge with Him!

Imagine how much better life on the Earth would be if all people of our planet became acquainted with this knowledge!

* * *

So, the first step on the path of mastering the art of meditation is attunement to the subtle and the beautiful, to BEAUTY!

The second step implies mastering the functions of the spiritual heart. We discuss this subject in detail in our other articles and books, for example in *Ecopsychology*. Therefore, here I will dwell on it only briefly.

The spiritual heart can start to develop in the anahata chakra located in the chest. Then, if one makes necessary spiritual efforts, it can grow larger than the anahata, than the entire body — and can continue to grow, can become as large as the size of our planet or even larger!

In the process of such development of the spiritual heart, the practitioner moves with the consciousness into it and becomes it.

And only in the multidimensional *depths* of such a developed spiritual heart, which encompasses the space above and below the surface of our planet, as well as around the planet, the practitioner can gain direct cognition of the Creator!

* * *

Perhaps, you already know that in previous years we created, tested, published, and even demonstrated in video films a very effective system of psychical self-regulation. Its course began with learning the theoretical fundamentals, including the ethical principles suggested to us by God. Then students had to master the techniques of relaxation and psycho-physical exercises, which created appropriate conditions for the transformation of the emotional sphere and allowed one to purify the energy structures of the organism. This produced a healing effect even at the early stages of mastering this system and allowed one to get rid of many diseases. Then the chakras and main meridians were purified and developed with the help of special methods, which resulted, among other things, in further improvement of the health of the body and soul. During the course, much attention was paid to strengthening the body (this included winter swimming), to communing with nature, to attunement to the beautiful. The main emphasis was always put on the development of the spiritual hearts.

After all, it is only developed spiritual hearts that allow us to make the states of pure and altruistic love steadfast and volitionally reproducible under any circumstance, even in difficult ones. And this ensured paradise (at least) for all those who managed to achieve these states during classes and retained them after the course.

But some students… abandoned these prospects. For example, some of them tried to "become again like everyone else" — and drank a glass of champagne at a celebration… But such meditative work is incompatible with drinking alcohol and taking any other narcotics, and everyone knew this. Some other students returned to non-vegetarian nutrition.

Killing-free nutrition (the one based on vegetal and milk products and on eggs) is the only correct diet for all people. The main reasons for this are two:

The first one is ethical. Love — as a state of the soul and way of life — is incompatible with the killing of animals for the sake of satisfaction of one's egoistic gluttony!

The second one is bioenergetical contamination. Many souls of killed animals enter the bodies of people who killed or ate them. These souls can feel very offended and sometimes want revenge. Such souls-possessors are called imps or demons. They can cause various somatic diseases and mental disorders.

(About other kinds of negative consequences of non-vegetarian nutrition and about how to choose an optimal diet, one can read in our books, for example in *Ecopsychology*).

… Why am I talking about this now? In order to illustrate the idea that it can be very harmful to teach the practical component of the spiritual science to those who are not mature yet from the ethical standpoint…

* * *

Now let us come back to the subject of development of the spiritual heart.

To do this work most effectively, one first needs to cleanse the anahata chakra. This is achieved with the help of special energy influences on the chakra.

For example, the practitioner introduces into the chakra (from the back) the image of a white tetrahedron rotating rapidly counterclockwise. This technique can be likened to removing decay from a tooth with the help of a dental drill.

Another method is to introduce into the chakra (already purified by the tetrahedron) the sound of the mantra "ya-a-a-a-m", which is sung softly and gently.

Then one can also introduce into the anahata images of beautiful fragrant flowers, such as roses or lilies-of-the-valley. Also one can listen to the spring singing of birds sounding in the chakra — such birds as robins, tits, or other gentle singers.

When the chakra becomes pure and large, we have to learn to perceive ourselves (as souls) entirely inside it — and to push the walls of the chakra from inside with the help of the hands of the soul. First, we practice pushing one wall after another, then — all walls in all directions simultaneously. Thus we begin to expand the chakra.

We must also learn to *look* from within the anahata. Let me emphasize that in the beginning one learns to *look*, not to *see*. The ability to see comes later.

We have to learn to *look* from the anahata not only forward but also backward; this is very important.

There is an exercise performed in pairs of adepts who help one another to learn to look back from the anahata. The first partner gently strokes the anahata area on the back of the second partner, drawing with his or her finger numbers or letters, and the second partner tries to recognize them. Then the partners exchange roles.

This useful and pleasant game can appeal even to young children. The memory of such games will help them develop their anahatas when they grow up.

... If one is not even able to enter with the consciousness into the anahata and to remain in it, then he or she should pay attention to purification of the other chakras, in particular the chakras of the head. Contamination of the head chakras attaches the consciousness to them and does not allow it to move into the anahata.

It can also be helpful to practice the psycho-physical exercises described in our books and demonstrated in our films.

* * *

Why do we need to learn to look back from the anahata chakra?

The point is that by always looking forward, we become used to seeing only material objects.

And by looking backward, we get rid of this stereotype. Moreover, when we look backward from the anahata, our indriyas of the vision of the soul go through the refining meridian called *chitrini*. And this makes it easier for us to learn to see inside subtle eons, which are close to the Abode of the Creator.

If one cannot do it, then one has to cleanse the meridians, especially the sushumna and chitrini.

* * *

And then one can continue training, doing it in nature by filling with *oneself-anahata* the energy *cocoons* of trees. For this task, one should choose healthy and strong trees that are not located in the thicket. Let me note that oak trees are not suitable for this purpose: their energy is unfavorable for refinement of the consciousness. It is best to seek plants favorable for this work among spring birches (biological species is betula pubescens), also among spruces, pines, larches, poplars, etc.

Then we expand — as spiritual hearts — above the expanse of the sea or above big lakes, above the steppe, above the mountains...

We can also invite to our anahatas Jesus Christ and other Divine Teachers — the Holy Spirits.

We learn to see Their giant Forms of Consciousness — Mahadoubles, consisting of the *Divine Light* invisible to the usual human eyesight.

Thus, little by little, month after month, year after year — we get closer to the state when we become able to perceive (i.e. to see, to hear) the Holy Spirits, to speak with Them, to merge with Them in Their Mahadoubles. Then They become personal Teachers for those who have reached this level of development.

But this is not the limit of our opportunities of spiritual growth. The next task is to reach the Abode of the Creator, from where the Holy Spirits come to help us, incarnate people.

* * *

One of the possible ways to continue advancement is the situation when the non-incarnate Divine Teacher brings His or Her disciples to Mergence with the Primordial Consciousness — through His or Her Mahadouble. In other words, the disciple merges with the Beloved Teacher and gradually grows with the consciousness inside Him or Her, becoming similar to the Teacher in the quality and in the size of the soul. Having filled so the Mahadouble of the Teacher, the disciple continues to grow — now in the Abode of the Creator, from where the Teacher's Mahadouble comes.

Probably, in this way Disciples of such Teachers as Krishna and Jesus achieved the fullness of Perfection and became Divine.

But we were led by God in a different way in order to have the opportunity to more broadly cognize the human possibilities of growth at these stages of development and, so to speak, *the anatomy of God.*

In particular, we have become acquainted with many Divine Teachers. They all have the same — Divine — level of refinement of the Consciousness; They all come out from the same Abode. But almost every One of Them walked the Path to Perfection — with individual variations. Their biographies are described in our book *Classic of Spiritual Philosophy and the Present* — and now everyone walking the Path to the Creator can use Their rich experience.

* * *

Let me tell you also about how we were led to the state of Nirodhi.

We were taught the mechanism of "dissolution" of oneself (as a consciousness) — long before we began to learn to merge with the Holy Spirits and with the Primordial Consciousness. It happened thanks to mastering the state of *total reciprocity* at special *places of power.* Moreover, our Divine Teachers showed us these places in such an order that we, knowing nothing of the mechanism of achieving the state of Nirodhi, could gradually and slowly comprehend the material in "small doses".

To make it more clear, I should add that we had no incarnate Teacher Who could explain everything to us in an easy-to-understand language. From the very beginning and up to the present day, we have been guided by non-incarnate Representatives of the Creator.

… So, let me repeat that the phenomenon of *total reciprocity*, which eventually leads to realization of the state of Nirodhi, was taught to us by demonstrating its mechanism first in small volumes of space and then gradually in much larger scales, up to the universal scale.

Why do I speak so much about this? Because it is very difficult — to teach *total reciprocity!* It cannot be done only with the use of words! It is so unusual: from the normal state of feeling the "I" — to enter the state of "non-I"! How is it possible to exist as "non-I"? How can one learn to change easily, at any moment, from "I" — to "non-I", and vice versa?

But now it is easy for us to do. Look: (demonstration of the meditation). When I do this, you see that nothing happens with my body: for example, I can sit, stand, walk, talk… Even my facial expression does not change…

Why is this needed? In order that having cognized God in His Universal Greatness, one could easily enter the state of Mergence with Him, in other words, the state of Nirvana.

And why does it make sense to teach "the disappearance of oneself" so early, as it was done in our case? Because this pedagogical method confidently suppresses the possibility of development of pride and self-admiration in students — on the grounds of personal achievements!

* * *

I want to tell you also about how we studied the structure of the Absolute.

Yes, our Teachers showed to us all the eons of the Absolute. But it was not an easy task — to arrange all of them in a logical sequence, in the form of a chart. They "refused" to be arranged as a simple sequence on the "steps" of the scale of *subtlety-coarseness!*

Their relative positions, in fact, turned out to be more complex! (I am talking about the chart for studying the structure of the Absolute presented in the book *Ecopsychology*).

So, how should one work with this chart?

Of course, first of all one must master everything that precedes this stage of work on oneself.

Then (preferably at special *places of power*), we exit from the bottom part of the anahata in the backward and slightly downward direction — and then we find ourselves in a space of soft and gentle calm, resembling the harmony of a warm southern night with many stars seen everywhere around. This is the eon of protoprakriti: a universal "storage" of elementary particles intended for construction of material objects, including stars and planets. This is one of the behind-the-Mirror eons.

By the way, what is the origin of the term *behind-the-Mirror?*

A usual material mirror has two sides: the front side, which is light (when it is lighted), and the back side, which is dark.

In the cosmic multidimensional reality — the *Mirror* is a membrane invisible to the ordinary sight, which divides a group of eons. One can find this *Mirror* behind one's own anahata chakra.

In front of our material bodies we see light (daylight or artificial), but having passed through the *Mirror*, we come to a space where there is no bright light. This is why the terms *Mirror* and *behind-the-Mirror* were chosen to describe these phenomena.

... If we go down behind the *Mirror* to the *multidimensional depths*, we come to two other eons — with increasing brightness. They, too, have to be explored. But we must not settle in them forever.

We should also explore all the other eons shown on the above-mentioned chart, of course, except of hell.

... In order not to raise doubts about the credibility of this chart, let me explain the following:

This concerns the relationship between the objective and the subjective.

Eons, which we are talking about now, exist objectively, i.e. they exist independent of the existence or non-existence of the subject or subjects, and independent of the subject's opinions.

But at the same time, a person exploring these eons becomes convinced that if he or she fills these eons with themselves (as the consciousnesses), then they all will move and rotate together with the material body of this person…

So, what does it mean? Self-deception? An illusion of perception?

No. The point is that the chart shows just entrances into eons, not the eons themselves. Moreover, each of us, people, from birth has this "construction" "attached" to the body. This is our potential that we can use or not use during the time of earthly incarnations. Namely, everyone has a choice:

— to remain in the world of matter (prakriti) if one devotes the entire life to it and becomes attached to it,

— or to go to hell if one cultivates emotional coarseness (or indulges in the already existing ones),

— or to dedicate life to studying the eons of the Absolute with emphasis placed on the most subtle of them, including the eon from where the Representatives of the Creator come to.

In relation to what was said above, it is appropriate to recall the biblical statement that man was made in God's image. But this likeness has nothing to do with bodily appearance. It concerns the multidimensional structure of the Absolute — and the multidimensional *potential* of each of us, which we discuss now.

… When we master the three eons behind the *Mirror*, it may seem to us that the deepest one of them is the Abode of the Creator. But it is not true. This eon is just an aggregate of the Atmic potentials of people. In other words, one can say that here everyone can find his or her Main Components (potential or already realized) — the Atmans.

But Paramatman (the Divine Atman, the main Essence of the Absolute, the Primordial Consciousness, the Creator, God-the-Father, Allah, Ishvara, Tao, Turiya) is found between two such Atmic structures.

It is for this purpose that one has to master them both — on the right and on the left...

* * *

So, in our conversation today I had the task of briefly describing the most important steps of the Path of spiritual self-realization of man. In the beginning, we discussed how one makes the first attempts to "open up" the spiritual heart, and in the end — how one can cognize the Creator in His Abode and merge with Him.

You probably noticed that there are stages of development that I have not talked about. For example, it is the information about Kundalini, about the vertical segments, about the *United We*, about the "Sun of God", about how to divinize the matter of the body. Why? Because it would require more time. But all such important information can be found in our other articles and books.

At the end of my talk, I want to ask you not to think that all the described stages can be mastered quickly! On the contrary, one has to dedicate the entire life to this!

I wish you success!

Be Careful!

In book [13] we described, among other things, how people pervert the Teachings of God. Such things happened in the past and continue to happen now.

One of the causes of such perversions consists in the incompetence of translators. For example, there are highly perverted translations of the Bhagavad Gita and Tao Te Ching. The same thing can be observed now with the translations of the books of Sathya Sai Baba (and books about Him).

Therefore I have to advise readers to be careful when reading these books; it is especially important with the translation of certain terms.[28]

For example, some translators, incapable of comprehending information from Sathya Sai Baba, translated the word *buddhi* as "intellect" — in contrast to the mind (*manas*). It may look reasonable: some people have a lesser *mind* — while others have a large developed *intellect!*...

But such an error in translation completely destroys the large methodological importance of the theme of development of buddhi, and of entire Buddhi Yoga in general!

Reading about the contrast between the mind and the intellect, what use can the reader find in such ideas? None!

Some may even think in a lofty way about themselves: I have an intellect! While they...

... Even worse consequences were caused by incompetent attempts to translate the word *Atman*. This term literally means "non-darkness", that is the Divinely Shining Main Essence of man, which everyone has to cognize in order to merge then with Paramatman, i.e. with the Primordial Consciousness, with the Creator.

Some English-speaking translators, who had no idea about the higher stages of the methodology of spiritual development, instead of keeping this unclear term non-translated (i.e. just writing *Atman*), translated it into English as *Self*.

And those who translated these texts from English into Russian made this absurd tendency even worse: they translated it as Selfhood!

---

[28] We discussed this subject also in [8,9].

So it turned out that God suggests to us to develop selfhood! Hurray!...

... Thus the translation was interpreted as the opposite meaning! The term *selfhood* may denote viciously inflated self-appraisal, haughtiness, inflated lower self!

But God teaches the opposite: to destroy selfhood in ourselves! It is absolutely necessary for cognition of the Atman and in general for making progress on the spiritual Path!

... Those who created and published such ignorant translations apparently believed that they do a good thing... While in reality it turned out that they perverted the Teachings of God to the opposite!

No wonder that many reasonable people, after reading such texts, refused these Teachings and decided that this is nothing more than another ridiculous and harmful sect...

... In Sanskrit there is also the term *viveka* denoting the ability to discern between true and false.

Ramakrishna named one of his disciples *Vivekananda*, that means Blissful One Possessing Viveka.

On the Path to Bliss attained in Mergence with the Primordial Consciousness we necessarily have to master viveka!

I wish you success!

The Straight Path

The term *Straight Path* can be found, among other sources, in Tao Te Ching (53), in the New Testament (2 Peter 2:15), in the Quran (2:136, 2:257, 2:266, 28:50), in the Teachings of Buddhism, and in the Teachings of Sathya Sai [8 and others]. These words imply the possibility for the fastest realization of the Creator's Intention for every one of us. This Intention can be expressed in the clearest and most concise way by the words of Jesus Christ: "... be perfect, as your Heavenly Father is perfect" (Matthew 5:48).

All those, who are involved — in one way or another — in the theme of spiritual development, should remember that an ethical component is the basis for this development. You can find abundant information about this in [8-9], among other books, and in other materials that are mentioned at the end of this publication.

Now let us focus on the intellectual interpretation of the term *Straight Path* and on the psychoenergetical component of spiritual work.

Understanding of the Straight Path

For the successful realization of the Straight Path, it is necessary, first of all, to accept the existence of One Universal God-Absolute.

One should not seek Him on some other planet, on some mountain or in some human-made temple on the Earth. He is not only present high above our material bodies that live on the round Earth but also everywhere. Yet one can find Him only through the development of oneself as a spiritual heart.

God in the Aspect of the Absolute is one Universal and multi-layered (multidimensional) Macroorganism. His layers (called *eons* in Greek and *lokas* in Sanskrit) do not differ by their "three-dimensional" parameters but by the degree of their subtlety or coarseness.

We can speak about two such scales of the real multidimensionality.

The first one of them is the degrees of density of energies between the Creator — and His material Creation.

The second one is between the Creator — and the border of hell, which is the "rubbish heap" of the Evolution.

Hell is the "abode" of the coarsest (by their emotional status) souls.

On the contrary, the Primordial Consciousness, Which is also called the Creator, God-the-Father, Allah, Ishvara, Tao, Odin, Svarog, Rod, and by other names in different human languages, is the subtlest Manifestation of the Absolute and Its Essence.

I want to stress once again that when we talk about the process of becoming subtler or coarser that the consciousness (soul) undergoes, we are talking about the change of its most typical emotional status. It is so because emotions are the states of us as souls.

Hence it follows that the path to hell is traversed through becoming coarser emotionally.

The Path to the Creator, on the contrary, is the consistent refinement of one's own emotional status.

In other words, we can say that the Path to the Creator is the advancement into the *depth* of the Absolute by the *scale of coarseness-subtlety*, while the path to hell is the same advancement by this scale but towards the *outside*.

Let me remind you that Jesus described hell as the "outer darkness" (Matthew 8:12).

The scheme for the initial study of the structure of the Absolute was published by us many times [9 and others]. Seven main spatial dimensions, including hell, are represented on it.

Those, who have explored — through meditative work — the Absolute in the perspective that is represented on this scheme, may be able to cognize the principal states of the Primordial Consciousness as well: they are *Calm* in the Abode of the Creator and different states of the Holy Spirits Who come out from it. These states vary in their intensity from the Divine *Light* — to the modifications of the Divine *Fire*.

* * *

God is really interested in our spiritual development, because those of us, who attain the Perfection on this Path, enrich Him with ourselves, having flowed into Him.

Therefore, the study and the fulfillment of God's Will for us is righteousness before Him, while the rejection to fulfill it — is a karmically punishable vice.

Spiritual Heart

I can affirm with confidence that the ancient precepts of the Hesychasts (those who sought inner silence and obtained it in the *depths* of their spiritual hearts [9 and others]) are indeed correct.

It is not by other means but through the development of the spiritual heart that one can attain the paradisiacal states of the soul during the life of one's material body — and then to remain in paradise after the end of one's incarnation.

Further self-development in this direction — through the stage of the transformation of oneself into the giant spiritual heart — can result in the real cognition of God in all His main Manifestations and in the Mergence with the Creator in His Abode.

We have explained specific methods for the initial development of the spiritual heart in several books [9 and others] and showed them in films. Therefore, I will not dwell at length on this issue now.

Let me just note, for those, who have never before been engaged in serious spiritual work, that one should not look for the spiritual heart in the material heart, or on the left of it, or in the spine, or in the stomach (some people even invented this). In reality, the spiritual heart starts growing in the anahata chakra, which is located in the chest, to be precise below the collarbones up to the "solar plexus". So, among the organs of the body, the anahata coincides, first of all, with the lungs, while the material heart is located on the border between the anahata and the manipura and is influenced by both of these chakras. On the one hand, its functional state can be influenced by the calm of the purified and developed loving anahata. On the other hand, it can be influenced by negative states that "boil" in the manipura, which was not regulated through the methods of psychical self-regulation [9]. Thus we gain health — or psychosomatic diseases of our material hearts.

... So in the beginning, it is necessary to cleanse the anahata chakra of bio-energetic contaminations and expand it so that it fills the entire chest. Then we should learn to look from it in all directions with the eyes of the soul, to listen and to speak, maintaining at the same the concentration of the consciousness inside.

Vocalists can easily master the skills of "pectoral" singing in this way.

All other people, who have learned to speak "from the anahata", also become much more welcome interlocutors. Even just silent communication with "anahatic" people gives calm and peace in contrast to the communication with the representatives of ajnic or ajnic-manipuric psychotypes.

The methods for the development of the spiritual heart can be mastered by a great number of people, including children [7-9], and this will allow them, when they grow up, to have better possibilities of mastering the heights of the spiritual Path.

It will be beneficial to conduct respective classes with children not only in closed spaces like halls or rooms but also in the midst of the harmony of nature. The courses of such classes — provided that ethical vital standards are observed — result, among other things, in the radical improvement of the health of the participants.

... Then we can continue to grow being the soul that consists of the spiritual heart. Thus we become bigger and bigger than our material bodies [9].

Only the consciousness that was refined in this way becomes able to perceive the Holy Spirits directly: to see Them, to attune with Them as the Standards of the Divine Subtlety, to embrace Them and to merge with Them. Thus we really cognize that God is indeed Perfect Love (1 John 4:8).

Jesus, Krishna, Babaji from Haidakhan, Sathya Sai and many Others [8-10] become our real Divine Teachers Who lead Their worthy disciples to a more and more complete cognition of God.

When we establish the closest mutual contact with the Holy Spirits, Who become easily perceived and turn into our beloved Friends and Teachers Who also love us, we will be able to learn from Them in the most fruitful way.

In this case, we can understand, by observing Their facial expressions, for example, if They are joking or speaking quite seriously.

In contrast to such relations with Them, there can be cases in which some people just "hear voices". But these "voices" can belong to anyone... That is why it is wrong to trust, without serious critical evaluation, the information that is received from such people.

... Let me stress once again that the aspiration for the maximum ethical purity should always be a dominating idea for all those who seek to progress on the Straight Path. Otherwise, God begins to laugh and play jokes on such negligent disciples, for example, by tempting them into realizing absurd actions. What is the meaning of this? The meaning is to show these people and others around them that one should not behave in this way!

Mergence

The cognition of God is possible only against the background of intense love for Him.

It is so, because the emotions of sincere love are what bring consciousnesses together.

God can easily see any falsity in our emotions.

He Himself is Perfect Love; therefore, He does not allow those, who have defects in their love, to approach Him.

We are completely naked — in our actions, emotions, and thoughts — before Him, Who is observing every one of us from the depths of the multidimensionality.

God is not "somewhere out there" but directly *under* the cells of our bodies and *under* every one of us as souls. He sees, hears, and feels everyone in every moment; on the contrary, people usually do not perceive Him...

... Many people believe that love only consists of the things that are related to sex and that jealousy is an indicator of the intensity of love...

However, the truth is opposite. When such people speak about love, they usually mean sexual passion, which it would be better to get rid of.

There is also a word *lust*, which means a strong sexual desire.

But true love is the opposite of lust and means to *give* oneself and one's things to the beloved ones. It can manifest itself, among other areas, in the area of sexual relations. However, it should not contain even a shadow of jealousy! Jealousy originates from a proprietary attitude towards another person, whom a jealous one perceives as an object for the satisfaction of his or her lust!

Jealousy and selfish violence are striking and gross manifestations of vicious egocentrism!

Selflessness and self-sacrifice are, on the contrary, the signs of true love, that love which God wants to see in us.

* * *

So what is the fastest way to master real love?

Of course, it is necessary to use intellectual self-examination, including repentance.

Besides, this process can be radically accelerated with the help of special methods for the development of the spiritual heart.

Nevertheless, no psychological techniques will give a lasting effect if one does not dedicate one's life to the good of all other incarnate beings who are worthy of it and to God.

It is appropriate to learn to give selflessly in sexual relations [4], in the upbringing of children [7], and in helping animals and plants, including those that live in the wild.

That person, who does not have a developed ability to love, cannot fall in love with God.

Such a person will not be able give himself or herself to God!

To achieve the Mergence with God, one should strive to eradicate one's own egocentrism completely.

Besides, on the higher stages of the Path, it is necessary to master the state of "non-I", in which one — during meditative trainings — only perceives transparent *emptiness* in that place where the feeling of *oneself* was before; the "I" in this case flows completely into the Divine Consciousness and merges with It.

It is appropriate to prepare oneself for this in everyday life among other people, and this is what Jesus also teaches us [8]. The next stages are explained, among other sources, in our books and relevant films.

... After learning to stay in the subtlest Components of the Absolute and after the real cognition of Its Infinite Greatness — it becomes quite easy for us to subdue our egos completely. No matter how big is one's self-awareness, when one realizes the Infinite Vastness of God in comparison with oneself, one sincerely surrenders by eliminating one's "I" through flowing into Him.

Afterwards, the Mergence becomes stronger and stronger, and such a practitioner masters His functions...

The "Star of David" and a Pentagram

Unfortunately, only very few people will be able to fulfill soon what we are going to discuss in this article. For the rest, let this information play its role in the future.

Why is it so? Because we will speak about the higher stages of spiritual development, and there are only very few people who are on them now.

Let us examine very briefly the main stages of the spiritual Path.

1. Initially, it is necessary to try to understand the essence of the organization of the Absolute and of Its Evolution.

2. Then one should bring oneself as close as possible to the standard of ethical purity, as God understands it.

3. Then one should cleanse one's body of energy contaminations, "open" the anahata chakra, and become — with the help of the methods of the modern, developed Hesychasm — a spiritual heart growing outside the body.

4. Then one should learn to turn off the mind during meditative trainings (Without this, all attempts to meditate will result only in the play of the mind, in the useless fantasies).

5. Then one should master, among other things, the set of meditations under the general topic "Pyramid". Here

the variants can be "Volcano" and then "Temple". These two are more convenient for the initial mastering. Afterwards, it will be more suitable to work with "Cone".

6. Then one should cognize God in His different Aspects and learn to merge with the Holy Spirits — in Their individual Manifestations and in Their *United We;*

7. Then one should become the spiritual heart that is oceanic by its size and that exists in the Divine Light and in the Light-Fire. It is also important to achieve the stability in the subtle states of the consciousness and maintain them even under adverse circumstances.

Only after this the time comes to use the meditations that are encoded in the symbols mentioned in the title of this article.

These symbols came to us from ancient Atlantis, but their true meaning was forgotten by people.

From a certain time, people began to use them as the state symbols of some countries.

Some occultists tried to interpret them quite simplistically. For example, they saw the contours of a human body with outstretched arms and legs in the pentagram (a five-pointed star), and the "Star of David" (hexagram, a six-pointed star) was considered by them as a symbol of a sexual union.

However, is there any usefulness from such interpretations?

… Thoth-the-Atlantean (Hermes Trismegistus in His subsequent Incarnation), Who is the creator of these symbols, explains that one should see them as the images of the pyramids (or cones) that should be filled — on a macroscale — with the developed individual consciousness. Moreover, these pyramidal forms of the consciousness are only the small part of such a soul, while the main volume of it should be spread outside the wide end of the pyramids — in the Mergence with the Divine Light of the *United We* of the Holy Spirits.

There are also the images of the almost horizontal pyramids in a pentagram; it is necessary to do the same with them.

Besides, the images of the pyramids symbolize the vectors of the direction of the attention or of the movement of the components of the consciousness that are included in pyramids.

In a pentagram, its vertical component means the initial distribution of the consciousness for this meditation. This is an *Enlightened* Person, that is, the One Who really consists of the Divine *Light*.

Then we superpose the two (and then even more) horizontal components, which signify the vectors directed from the outside — towards the center. The consciousness moves into them completely. These structures of the consciousness touch one another and then interpenetrate. The anterior "I", which was in the center and which was located in the body, disappears, being "washed away", and only God remains in the Aspect of the *United We* of the Holy Spirits.

We mastered this meditative principle in another way. We did not use this graphic scheme but natural means and the direct guidance of the Divine Teachers — the Holy Spirits. This is how others can also master this.

In other words, a pentagram just symbolizes a principle of Mergence of the developed individual consciousness — with the *United We* of the Holy Spirits. And to find the steps towards this Goal is the task that is carried out in the specific religious associations.

... Now let us examine the essence of a hexagram.

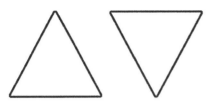 

It symbolizes the union of the two mentioned "pyramids of the consciousness" in the layer of the subtlest Divine Light-Fire, and it is realized *under* the matter of one's body. This allows one to look at one's own body (in order to transform it) from the position of God and being in the Mergence with Him.

The volume of space, in which this meditation is done, corresponds approximately to the scale of our planet. In this respect, let me remind you that the Author of the examined symbols recommended to cognize the layer (eon, loka) of the Divine Light both "above" and "below" relative to the Earth [8].

Besides, a practitioner should have the already developed arms of the consciousness, with the help of which he or she can easily move in space and exert influence on different objects.

... On the Internet, there is a very useful illustration of the relation between a pentagram and a hexagram: a pentagram is inside, in the center of an incomparably greater hexagram. The creator of this scheme really understood the essence!

 In conclusion, I want to ask my readers not to try to perform these meditations before all previous stages of spiritual growth have been mastered. These stages are mentioned in this article and

examined in more detail in our other publications and films.

It also should be well understood that one cannot approach (by the state of the soul) the Primordial Consciousness with the help of such methods without Its consent and full approval for this in a given moment.

God can begin to make fun of those who are not worthy of approaching Him yet (for example, by an ethical criterion) and sometimes even to "throw them down from the stairs".

So, let us strive for the Goal and at the same time be cautious and careful in evaluating our own worthiness before Him!

Meditation of Radomir "Absolute"

Radomir, Who is mentioned in this article, was a spiritual Master in His last incarnation and contributed to the spiritual development of several of His incarnated disciples, Who reached then the Divine Perfection and Who manifest Themselves now as the Holy Spirits. Their names are Rada, Alexey and Eremey. You can find Their biographies in [8].

The meditation that we will describe in this article and that is proposed by Radomir is one of the highest on the stages of the spiritual ascent. That is why not everyone will be able to perform it right now. This meditation is not an image created by the mind in the head, but the variant of the distribution, in the multidimensional space, of the consciousness that has been developed to a significant degree on the previous stages of the spiritual growth. Namely, speaking in a very general outline, one should fulfill the following before being able to perform this meditation:

a) to purify the body and the consciousness that lives in it,

b) to become a huge spiritual heart that greatly exceeds the size of the material body,

c) to develop the arms of the consciousness that allow one, among other things, to move in the multidimensional space,

d) to learn to merge with the Divine Consciousness by dissolving in It, in the cognized and mastered subtlest layers of the Absolute.

We have examined all this in detail on the pages of our books and in our films.

* * *

The essence of the examined meditation is the following:

It is necessary to feel the Absolute as an infinite by its size and multidimensional Ball. Its layers are inserted one into another, and each subtler layer is located closer to the center of this Ball. Denser layers, on the contrary, are located closer to the periphery, and the coarsest ones of them are outside of this Ball; this is the "outer darkness" of which Jesus spoke (Matthew 8:12).

In the center of this Ball, there is Its Core — "the Heart of the Absolute" — that is, Its most important Part in Its active state. This is one of the main Manifestations of the Primordial Consciousness, Which is also called the Creator, God-the-Father, Allah, Tao, Svarog, etc. in different human languages. It is perceived as the Living, Loving and Tenderest Divine Fire, Which invites worthy spiritual practitioners to flow into It forever. It is also One Universal Ocean of the Creator, Which is the *United We* of All Those Who have reached It.

The task of a spiritual practitioner is to establish a significant part of himself or herself as the developed consciousness in the center of this Ball and then to direct a Part of Himself or Herself to other layers of the Absolute (including the world of matter) in order to help embodied souls who live there. For example, one can create Mahadoubles and *working sites,* which facilitate the communication with these embodied souls and allow one to teach them concrete meditative techniques [9]. This is how the Holy Spirits and the Messiahs (Avatars) exist and act, among other ways.

* * *

For those who have already approached this stage of the development, the description of the meditation that is given in this article will help in mastering that stage. May it also help everyone else in the theoretical cognition of the *anatomy of God.*

God is quite cognizable. However, this is true only for those who have already developed themselves (ethically and intellectually) and who grow themselves as spiritual hearts. In relation to this, let me remind you of the words of Jesus: "Blessed are the pure in heart, for they will see God!" (Matthew 5).

On the contrary, for those who do not want to perfect themselves spiritually, God is indeed incognizable. It would be great that these people, having acquainted themselves with the real possibilities of the spiritual growth, begin to strive to become better before God Who really exists!

The materials listed in the bibliography in this book and in our other books explain how one can achieve this.

Recommended Literature

1. Antonov V.V. — The New Upanishad: Structure and Cognition of the Absolute. Saint Petersburg, "Polus", 1999 *(in Russian)*.
2. Antonov V.V. (ed.) — God Speaks. Textbook of Religion. "Polus", Saint Petersburg, 2002 *(in Russian)*.
3. Antonov V.V. (ed.) — Spiritual Heart: Path to the Creator (Poems-Meditations and Revelations). "New Atlanteans", Bancroft, 2007 *(in Russian)*.
4. Antonov V.V. — Sexology: Development and Regulation of the Reproductive Function. "New Atlanteans", Bancroft, 2009.
5. Antonov V.V. — How God Can Be Cognized. Autobiography of a Scientist Who Studied God. "New Atlanteans", Bancroft, 2009.
6. Antonov V.V. (ed.) — How God Can Be Cognized. Book 2. Autobiographies of God's Disciples. "New Atlanteans", Bancroft, 2008.
7. Antonov V.V. (ed.) — Spiritual Work with Children. "New Atlanteans", Bancroft, 2008.
8. Antonov V.V. (ed.) — Classics of Spiritual Philosophy and the Present. "New Atlanteans", Bancroft, 2008.
9. Antonov V.V. — Ecopsychology. "New Atlanteans", Bancroft, 2008.
10. Antonov V.V. (ed.) — Forest Lectures on the Highest Yoga. "New Atlanteans", Bancroft, 2008.
11. Antonov V.V. — The Bhagavad Gita with Commentaries. "New Atlanteans", Bancroft, 2008.
12. Antonov V.V. (ed.) — Tao Te Ching. "New Atlanteans", Bancroft, 2008.
13. Antonov V.V. — Spiritual Heart — Religion of Unity. "New Atlanteans", Bancroft, 2008.
14. Antonov V.V. — Life for God. "New Atlanteans", Bancroft, 2013.

15. Antonov V.V., Zubkova A.B. — Taoism. "New Atlanteans", Bancroft, 2013.
16. Castaneda C. — The Fire from Within. "Simon and Shuster", N.Y., 1984.
17. Cullen B. (comp) — The Book of Jesus. "Polus", Saint Petersburg, 1997 (*in Russian*).
18. Spalding B. — Life and Teaching of the Masters of the Far East. "DeVorss & Co", 1924.
19. Tatyana M. — On the Other Side of the Material World. "New Atlanteans", Bancroft, 2012.
20. Teplyy A.B. (comp.) — Book of the Warrior of Spirit. "New Atlanteans", Bancroft, 2008.
21. Way of Pilgrim. Kazan, 1911.
22. Zubkova A.B. — Story about Princess Nesmeyana and Ivan. "New Atlanteans", Bancroft, 2007.
23. Zubkova A.B. — Dobrynya. Bylinas. "New Atlanteans", Bancroft, 2008.
24. Zubkova A.B. — Dialogues with Pythagoras. "New Atlanteans", Bancroft, 2008.
25. Zubkova A.B. — Divine Parables. "New Atlanteans", Bancroft, 2008.
26. Zubkova A.B. (comp.) — Book of the Born in the Light. Revelations of the Divine Atlanteans. "New Atlanteans", Bancroft, 2008.
27. Zubkova A.B. — Parables of Lao Tse. «New Atlanteans», Bancroft, 2011.
28. Zubkova A.B. — Parables about the Elder Zosima. «New Atlanteans», Bancroft, 2013.
29. Zubkova A.B. — Divine Stories of Slavic Lands. "New Atlanteans", Bancroft, 2013.
30. Zubkova A.B. — Story about Knyaz Dmitry and Volhva. "New Atlanteans", Bancroft, 2013.

Our video films:

1. *Immersion into Harmony of Nature. The Way to Paradise.* (Slideshow), 90 minutes (on CD or DVD).
2. *Spiritual Heart.* 70 minutes (on DVD).
3. *Sattva* (Harmony, Purity). 60 minutes (on DVD).
4. *Sattva of Mists.* 75 minutes (on DVD).
5. *Sattva of Spring.* 90 minutes (on DVD).
6. *Art of Being Happy.* 42 minutes (on DVD).
7. *Keys to the Secrets of Life. Achievement of Immortality.* 38 minutes (on DVD).
8. *Bhakti Yoga.* 47 minutes (on DVD).
9. *Kriya Yoga.* 40 minutes (on DVD).
10. *Ecopsychology.* 60 minutes (on DVD).
11. *Yoga of Krishna.* 80 minutes (on DVD).
12. *Yoga of Buddhism.* 130 minutes (on DVD).
13. *Taoist Yoga.* 91 minutes (on DVD).
14. *Ashtanga Yoga.* 60 minutes (on DVD).
15. *Agni Yoga.* 76 minutes (on DVD).
16. *Yoga of Sathya Sai Baba.* 100 minutes (on DVD).
17. *Yoga of Pythagoras.* 75 minutes (on DVD).
18. *Psychical Self-Regulation.* 112 minutes (on DVD).

You may order our books at Lulu e-store:
http://stores.lulu.com/spiritualheart
and at Amazon:
http://astore.amazon.com/spiritual-art-20

You can also download for free our video films, screensavers, printable calendars, etc. from the site:
www.spiritual-art.info

See on the site www.swami-center.org our books, photo gallery, and other materials in different languages.

Our other websites:
www.philosophy-of-religion.org.ua
www.teachings-of-jesus-christ.org
www.pythagoras.name
www.atlantis-and-atlanteans.org
www.path-to-tao.info
www.new-ecopsychology.org
www.encyclopedia-of-religion.org
www.meaning-of-life.tv
www.highest-yoga.info

Design of
Ekaterina Smirnova

Made in United States
North Haven, CT
29 November 2021

11753166R00065